Hunt for the Southern Continent

New Zealand, 1774

JAMES COOK

Hunt for the Southern Continent

Edited by PHILIP EDWARDS

GREAT
JOURNEYS

TED SMART

PENGUIN BOOKS

Published by the Penguin Group
Penguin Books Ltd, 80 Strand, London WC2R ORL, England
Penguin Group (USA) Inc., 375 Hudson Street, New York, New York 10014, USA
Penguin Group (Canada), 90 Eglinton Avenue East, Suite 700, Toronto, Ontario, Canada M4P 2Y3
(a division of Pearson Penguin Canada Inc.)
Penguin Ireland, 25 St Stephen's Green, Dublin 2, Ireland (a division of Penguin Books Ltd)
Penguin Group (Australia), 250 Camberwell Road, Camberwell, Victoria 3124, Australia
(a division of Pearson Australia Group Pty Ltd)
Penguin Books India Pvt Ltd, 11 Community Centre, Panchsheel Park, New Delhi – 110 017, India
Penguin Group (NZ), 67 Apollo Drive, Rosedale, North Shore 0632, New Zealand
(a division of Pearson New Zealand Ltd)
Penguin Books (South Africa) (Pty) Ltd, 24 Sturdee Avenue, Rosebank, Johannesburg 2196, South Africa

Penguin Books Ltd, Registered Offices: 80 Strand, London WC2R ORL, England

www.penguin.com

First published by the Hakluyt Society 1955–67, in 4 volumes
The Journals of Captain Cook first published in Penguin Classics 1999
This extract published in Penguin Books 2007

3

Inside-cover maps by Jeff Edwards

Taken from the Penguin Classics edition *The Journals of Captain Cook*,
edited by Philip Edwards

Typeset by Rowland Phototypesetting Ltd, Bury St Edmunds, Suffolk
Printed in England by Clays Ltd, St Ives plc

ISBN: 978-0-141-02543-8

This edition produced for The Book People Ltd,
Hall Wood Avenue, Haydock, St. Helens, WA11 9UL

Contents

James Cook (1728–1779), having completed an enormously successful exploration of the South Pacific in 1771, returned the following year in search of the mythical 'southern continent'. Using the already-known New Zealand as a hub, Cook negotiated two looped voyages searching the Pacific waters. Cook's journals are a colourful and engrossing account of one man's ambition to explore the world and form relationships with exotic peoples, all told in his own distinctive style.

This selection encompasses the second and more extensive of these loops, where Cook describes his journeys beyond the Antarctic Circle, as well as his encounters with natives in Easter Island, Tahiti and Tonga. Cook's idiosyncratic spelling has been preserved.

November 1773 New Zealand

WEDNESDAY 24*th*. At 4 o'Clock in the Morning we unmoored with an intent to put to Sea, but the wind being Northerly or NE without and blew in strong pufs into the Cove so that we were obliged to lay fast. While we were unmooring, some of our old friends the Natives came to take their leave of us and after wards took all their effects into their Canoes and left the Cove, but the party which had been out on the late expedition remained, these some of the gentlemen viseted and found the heart [of a Maori youth] still remaining on the Canoe and the bowels and lungs lying on the beach, but the flesh they believed was all devoured.

THURSDAY 25*th*. At 4 o'Clock in the Morning we weighed with a light breeze out of the Cove which carried us no farther than betwen Motuara and Long-island where we were obliged to anchor, presently after a breeze sprung up at North with which we weighed and turned out of the Sound by 12 o'Clock . . .

The morning before we sailed I wrote a memorandum seting forth the time we arrived last here, the day we sailed, the rout I intended to take & such other information as I thought necessary for Captain Furneaux to know and buried it in a bottle under the root of a tree in the garden in the bottom of the Cove in such a manner that it must be found by any European who may put into the Cove. I however have not the least reason to think that it will ever fall into the hands of the person I intended it for, for it is hardly possible that Captain Furneaux can be in any part of New Zealand and I not have heard of him in all this time, nevertheless I was determined not to leave the country without looking for him where I thought it was most likely for him to be found; accordingly as soon as we were clear of the Sound I hauld over for Cape Teerawhitte and ran along the shore from point to point to Cape Pallisser fireing guns every half hour without seeing or hearing the least signs of what we were in search after . . .

The next Morning at day-light we made Sail round Cape Pallisser fireing guns as usual but saw not the least signs of the Adventure and therefore bore away for Cape Campbell on the other side of the Strait having a light breeze at NE. Soon after we discovered a smoak to the NE a little way in-land, it was improbable enough that this should be made by any of the Adventures crew, I however determined to put it out of all manner of doubt and accordingly hauled the wind again, we kept plying till 6 o'Clock in the evening, several hours after this smoke and every other sign of people disapeared. All the officers being unanimous of opinion that the Adventure could neither be stranded on the Coast or be in any of the Ports in this Country determined me to spend no more time in search of her, but to proceed directly to the Southward. I am under

[no] apprehensions for the safety of the Adventure nor can I even guess which way she is gone, the manner she was seperated from me and [not] coming to the rendezvouze has left me no grounds to form any conjectors upon, I can only suppose that Captain Furneaux was tired with beating against the NW winds and had taken a resolution to make the best of his way to the Cape of good hope, be this as it may I have no expectation of joining him any more.

[. . .]

[*The* Adventure, *much less able than the* Resolution *to cope with adverse weather conditions, was constantly defeated in her attempts to battle her way to Queen Charlotte Sound, and it was not until 30 November that she succeeded – five days after Cook had left. They found the bottle, but necessary repairs etc. meant that they were not ready to sail until 17 December. Then disaster struck. The cutter did not return from a mission, and Furneaux found that the crew had been killed by the Maoris. It was not until 23 December that they finally left. By the time they reached the vicinity of Cape Horn, neither the ship nor the crew, nor their provisions, were in good shape, and Furneaux made the best of his way to the Cape of Good Hope and to England, which he reached on 14 July 1774.*

Meanwhile Cook set off towards the Antarctic without a consort, claiming that no one was dejected at the prospect of proceeding on their own 'to the South or wherever I thought proper to lead them'. By the middle of December they had reached the ice.]

[December 1773]

WEDNESDAY 15*th*. *Therm.r. Noon* 31. *Winds WBN, NNW, & West. Course S* 60°15' *E. Dist. Sailed* 116 *Miles. Lat. in South* 65°52'. *Longde. in West Reck.g.* 159°20'. *Long. made from C. Pallisser* 25°19'. Fresh gales and thick Foggy weather with snow, except in the PM when we had some intervals of clear Weather in one of which we found the Variation to be 14°12' E. At 6 o'Clock double reefed the Top-sails and handed the Main sail and Mizen Top-sail. The Ice begins to increase fast, from Noon till 8 o'Clock in the evening we saw but two islands, but from 8 to 4 AM we passed fifteen, besides a quantity of loose Ice which we sailed through, this last increased so fast upon us that at 6 o'Clock we were obliged to alter the Course more to the East, having to the South an extensive feild of loose ice; there were several partitions in the feild and clear water behind it, but as the wind blew strong the Weather foggy, the going in among this Ice might have been attended with bad concequences, especially as the wind would not permit us to return. We therefore hauled to the NE on which course we had stretched but a little way before we found our selves quite imbayed by the ice and were obliged to Tack and stretch back to the SW having the loose field ice to the South and many large islands to the North. After standing two hours on this tack the wind very luckily veered to the westward with which we tacked and stretched to the Northward (being at this time in Lat 66°0' s) and soon got clear of all the loose ice but had yet many huge islands to incounter, which were so numerous that we had to luff for one and bear up for a nother. One of these mases was very near proving fatal to us, we had not weather[ed] it more than once or twice our length, had we not succeeded this circumstance could never have been related. According to the old proverb a miss is as good as a mile, but our situation requires more misses than we can expect, this together with the improbability of meeting with land to the South and the impossibility of exploreing it for the ice if we did find any, determined me to haul to the north. This feild or loose ice is not such as is usually formed in Bays or Rivers, but like such as is broke off from large Islands, round ill-shaped pieces from the size of a small Ship's Hull downwards, whilest we were amongest it we frequently, notwithstanding all our care, ran against some of the large pieces, the shoks which the Ship received thereby was very considerable, such as no Ship could bear long unless properly prepared for the purpose. Saw a great number of Penguins on an ice island and some Antartick Petrels flying about.

THURSDAY 16*th*. *Therm.r. Noon* 31 *to* 33. *Winds West, Calm, SE. Course N* 19½° *E. Dist. Sailed* 102 *Miles. Lat. in South* 64°16'. *Longd. in West Reck.g.* 158°0'. *Longd. made from C. Pallisser* 26°39'. Continued to stretch to the Northward with a very fresh gale at west which was attended with thick snow showers till 8 PM when the weather began to clear up and the gale to abate. At 6 o'Clock in the am it fell Calm and continued so till

10 when a breeze sprung up at SEBS with which we stretched to the NE. Weather dark and gloomy and very cold our sails and rigging hung with icicles for these two days past. At present but few ice islands in sight but have past a great many this last 24 hours.

[...]

TUESDAY 21*st. Therm.r. Noon* 33. *Winds NE. Course S 41° E. Dist. Sailed 70 Miles. Lat. in South* 66°50'. *Longde. in West Reck.g.* 66°50'. *Long. made C. Palliser* 38°11'. In the PM the wind increased to a strong gale attended with a thick fogg sleet and rain which constitutes the very worst of weather, our rigging was so loaded with ice that we had enough to do to get our Top-sails down to double reef. At 7 o'Clock we came the second time under the Polar Circle and stood to the SE till 6 o'Clock in the am when being in Lat 67°5' South, Longitude 145°49' West, the fogg being exceeding thick we came close aboard a large Island of ice and being at the same time a good deal embarrass'd with loose ice we with some difficulty wore and stood to the NW until Noon when the fogg being some what disipated we resumed our Course again to the SE. The ice islands we fell in with in the morning, for there were more than one, were very high and rugged terminating in many Peaks, whereas all those we have seen before were quite flat at top and not so high. A great Sea from the North. Grey Albatroses and a few Antarctick Petrels.

[...]

FRIDAY 24*th*. *Therm.r. Noon* 32. *Winds Northerly. Course S* 40° *W. Dist. Sailed* 9 *Miles. Lat. in South* 67°19'. *Longde. in West Reck.g.* 138°15'. *Long. made C. Pallisser* 46°24'. At 4 o'Clock in the PM as we were standing to the SE, fell in with such a vast quantity of field or loose ice as covered the whole Sea from South to East and was so thick and close as to obstruct our passage, the wind at this time being pretty moderate, brought to in the edge of this feild, hoisted out two boats and sent them to take some up, and in the mean time we slung several large pi[e]ces along side and hoisted them in with our tackles; by such time as the Boats had made two trips it was Eight o'Clock when we hoisted them in and made sail to the westward under double reef'd Top-sails and Courses, with the wind notherly a strong gale attended with a thick fog Sleet and Snow which froze to the Rigging as it fell and decorated the whole with icicles. Our ropes were like wires, Sails like board or plates of Metal and the Shivers froze fast in the blocks so that it required our utmost effort to get a Top-sail down and up; the cold so intense as hardly to be endured, the whole Sea in a manner covered with ice, a hard gale and a thick fog: under all these unfavourable circumstances it was natural for me to think of returning more to the North, seeing there was no probability of finding land here nor a possibility of get[ting] farther to the South and to have proceeded to the East in this Latitude would not have been prudent as well on account of the ice as the vast space of Sea we must have left to the north unexplored, a space of 24° of Latitude in which a large track of land might lie, this point could only be determined by makeing a stretch to the North. While we were takeing up the ice two of the Antarctick Petrels so often mentioned were shott; we were right in our conjectures in supposeing them of the Petrel tribe; they are about the size of a large pigeon, the feathers of the head, back and part of the upper side of the wings are a lightish brown, the belly and under side of the wings white, the tail feathers which are 10 in number are white tiped with brown. At the same time we got another new Petrel smaller than the former, its plumage was dark grey. They were both casting their feathers and yet they were fuller of them than any birds we had seen, so much has nature taken care to cloath them sutable to the climate in which they live. At this time we saw two or three Chocolate coloured Albatrosses with yellowish Bills, these as well as the Petrels above mentioned are no were seen but among the ice. The bad weather continuing without the least variation for the better which made it necessary for us to proceed with great caution and to make short boards over that part of the Sea we had in some measure made our selves accquainted with the preceeding day, we were continually falling in with large ice islands which we had enough to do to keep clear of.

SATURDAY 25*th*. *Therm.r. Noon* 34. *Winds NW. Course N* 48¼° *E. Dist. Sailed* 84 *Miles. Lat. in South* 66°23'. *Longde. in West Reck.g.* 135°7'. *Long. made C. Palliser* 49°32'. In the PM the wind veer'd more to the West, the gale abated and the sky cleared up and presented to our view the many islands of ice we had escaped during the Fog. At 6 o'Clock being in Latitude 67°0' s, Long^de the same as yesterday at noon, the variation was observed to be 15°26' East. As we advanced to the NE with a gentle gale at NW the ice increased so fast upon us that at Noon no less than 90 or 100 large islands were seen round us besides innumerable smaller pieces.[1]

SUNDAY *26th. Therm.r. 37. Winds NNW, Calm, WSW. Course N 66° E. Dist. Sailed 20 Miles. Lat. in South 65°15'. Longde. in West Reck.g. 134°22'. Long. made C. Pallisser 50°17'. Varn. 16°2' East.* At 2 o'Clock in the PM it fell calm, we had before preceived this would happen and got the ship into as clear a birth as we could where she drifted along with the ice islands and by takeing the advantage of every light air of wind was kept from falling foul of any one; we were fortunate in two things, continual day light and clear weather, had it been foggy nothing less than a miracle could have kept us clear of them, for in the morning the whole sea was in a manner wholy covered with ice, 200 islands and upwards, none less than the Ships hull and some more than a mile in circuit were seen in the compass of five miles, the extent of our sight, and smaller peices innumerable. At 4 in the AM a light breeze sprung up at WSW and

---

[1] The usual Christmas celebrations were observed, rather muted because (according to Forster) 'a great many people in the ship', including himself, were 'very ill'.

enabled us to Steer north the most probable way to extricate our selves from these dangers.

[...]

[January 1774]

TUESDAY 4*th. Therm.r. Noon* 46¼. *Winds Westerly. Course NBE. Dist. Sailed* 114 *Miles. Lat. in* 54°55'. *Longd. in West Greenwich Reck.g.* 139°4', *East C. Pallisser* 45°45'. Fresh gales and Clowdy with some Showers of Sleet. In the PM saw a few more of the small divers, and some small pieces of weed which appeared to be old and decayed and not as if it had lately been broke from rocks. I can not tell what to think of the divers, had there been more of them I should have thought them signs of the vicinity of land, as I never saw any so far from known land before, probably these few may have been brought out thus far to Sea by some Shoal of fish, such were certainly about us by the vast number of Blue Petrels and Albatrosses, all of which left us before the evening. As the wind seems now fixed in the western board, we shall be under a necessity of leaving unexplored to the west a space of Sea containing 40° of Longitude and 20° or 21° of Latitude, had the wind been favourable I intended to have run 15° or 20° of longitude to the west in the Latitude we are now in and back again to the East in the Latitude of 50° or near it, this rout would have so intersected the space above mentioned as to have hardly left room for the bare supposission of any large land lying there. Indeed as it is we have no reason to suppose that there is any for we have had now for these several days past a great swell from west and NW, a great sign we have not been covered by any land between these two points. In the AM saw some Pie bald porpuses.

[. . .]

THURSDAY 6*th. Therm.r.* 47. *Winds West, NW, & WSW. Course N* 36°45' *E. Dist. Sailed* 128 *Miles. Lat. in* 52°0'. *Longde. in W. Greenwh. Reck.g.* 135°32'. *Watch* 135°38', *East Cape Palliser* 49°7'. Very strong gales and excessive heavy squalls attended with rain. At 8 pm took in the Top-sails till 8 am when the gale being some what abated set them again close reef'd. At Noon loosed all the reefs out and bore away NE with a fresh gale at WSW, fair weather, the distance between us now and our rout to Otaheite being little more than two hundred leagues in which space it is not probable there can be any land, and it is less probable there can be any to the west from the vast high billows we now have from that quarter.

[. . .]

TUESDAY 11*th. Therm.r. Noon* 50. *Winds Westerly. Course N* 81° *E. Dist. Sailed* 103 *Miles. Lat. in South* 47°51'. *Longde. W. Greenwh. Reck.g.* 122°12'. *Watch* 122°17'307". *Long. EC. Palliser* 62°27'. Little wind continued most part of the PM. In the night it began to freshen, blew in Squalls attended with rain, afterwards the weather became clear and the wind sittled. At Noon being little more than two hundred Leagues from my track to Otaheite in 1769 in which space it was not probable any thing was to be found, we therefore hauled up SE with a fresh gale at SWBW.

WEDNESDAY 12*th. Therm.r. Noon* 56. *Winds SWBW to NWBN. Course S* 42°30'. *Dist. Sailed* 138 *Miles. Lat. in South* 49°32'. *Longd. W. Greenwh. Reck.g.* 119°52'. *Watch* 119°57'. *Long. E. C. Palliser* 64°47'. Fresh gales and pleasent weather. In the PM found the variation 2°34' East. The Westerly swell still continues. Very few birds seen and these such as are found all over the Ocean in these Latitudes. At Noon hauled more to the Southward.

[. . .]

THURSDAY 20*th. Therm.r.* 40. *Winds NE & Easterly. Course S* 21° *E. Dist. Sailed* 45 *Miles. Lat. in South* 62°34'. *Longde. in West Reck.g.* 116°24'. *Long. East C. Palliser* 68°15'. First part fresh gales and hazey with rain, remainder little wind and Mostly fair. At 7 PM saw a large piece of Weed. In the AM two ice islands one of which was very high terminating in a peak or like the Cupala of St Pauls Church, we judged it to be 200 feet high. A great Westerly swell still continues a probable certainty there is no land between us and the Meridian of 133½° which we were under when last in this Latitude.

[. . .]

TUESDAY 25*th. Therm.r. Noon* 42. *Winds WNW to North. Course SBW½W. Dist. Sailed* 109 *Miles. Lat. in*

South 65°24'. *Longd. in W. Greenwh. Reck.g.* 109°31', *East C. Palliser* 75°8'. *Varn. East* 19°27'. First part fresh breeze and clowdy, Middle hazy with Sleet and rain, latter a gentle breeze and pleasent weather and the air very warm considering the Latitude. Not a bit of ice to be seen, which we who have been so much used to it think a little extraordinary and causes various opinions and conjectures.

WEDNESDAY 26*th. Therm.r. Noon* 40. *Winds Northerly. Course South. Dist. Sailed* 72 *Miles. Lat. in South* 66°36'. *Longd. in W. Greenwh. Reck.g.* 109°31', *East C. Palliser* 75°8'. *Varn. East* 18°20'. Gentle breezes and Clowdy mild weather. At 6 PM Latitude 65°44' S. Variation p^r Azm^{uths} 19°27' E and at 7 AM being then in Latitude 66°20' the Variation was 18°20' East. At this time saw Nine Ice islands, the most of them small, several Whales and a few blue Petrels. At 8 o'Clock we came the third time within the Antarctick Polar Circle. Soon after saw an appearence of land to the East and SE, haul'd up for it and presently after it disappeared in the haze. Sounded but found no ground with a line of 130 fathom. A few whales & Petrels seen.

THURSDAY 27*th. Therm.r.* 37½. *Winds NE. Course S* 21°15' *E. Dist. Sailed* 83 *Miles. Lat. in South* 67°52'. *Longd. in W. Greenwh. Reck.g.* 108°15', *East C. Palliser* 76°24'. Little wind and foggy with rain and Sleet, at intervals fair and tolerable clear. Continued to stretch to the SE till 8 o'Clock am by which time we were assured our supposed land was vanished into clowds and therefore resumed our Course to the South. A smooth Sea, what little swell we have is from the NE. A few Blue Petrels, Black Sheer-waters and Mother Caries Chickens are all the Birds we see.

[. . .]

SATURDAY 29*th. Therm.r.* 36½. *Winds NE, NW, & NNE. Course S* 33° *E. Dist. Sailed* 30 *Miles. Lat. in South* 70°00′ *Obn. Longd. in W. Greenwh. Reck.g.* 107°27′. *Watch* 107°36′, *East C. Pallisser* 77°12′. *Varn. East* 22°41′. At 1 o'Clock in the PM fell in with some loose ice, brought-to, hoisted out two Boats and took a quantity on board; which done made sail to the NW not daring to stand to the South in so thick a fog which hindered us from seeing the extent or quantity of ice we were among. The wind was Variable between NW and North and but little of it. At Midnight Tacked to the Eastwards. At 4 o'Clock the Sky cleared up, the wind fixed at NNE and we bore away SSE passing several large Ice islands. Betwixt 4 and 8 o'Clock found the variation by several trials to be 22°41′ E. Latitude at this time about 69°45′ S. Clear pleasent Weather, Air not cold.

SUNDAY 30*th. Winds ESE. Course S* 20° *E. Dist. Sailed* 51 *Miles. Lat. in South* 70°48′. *Longd. in W. Reck.g.* 106°34′. Continued to have a gentle gale at NE with Clear pleasent weather till towards the evening, when the Sky became Clowded and the air Cold atten[d]ed with a smart frost. In the Latitude of 70°23′ the Variation was 24°31′ East; some little time after saw a piece of Rock Weed covered with Barnacles which one of the brown Albatroses was picking off. At 10 o'Clock pass'd a very large Ice island which was not less than 3 miles in circuit, presently after came on a thick fog, this made it unsafe to stand on, especially as we had seen more Ice Islands ahead; we therefore tacked and made a trip to the North for about one hour and a half in which time the fog dissipated and we resumed our Cou[r]se to the SSE, in which rout we met with several large ice islands. A little after 4 AM we precieved the Clowds to the South near the horizon to be of an unusual Snow white brightness which denounced our approach to field ice, soon after it was seen from the Mast-head and at 8 o'Clock we were close to the edge of it which extended East and West in a streight line far beyond our sight; as appear'd by the brightness of the horizon; in the Situation we were now in just the Southern half of the horizon was enlightned by the Reflected rays of the Ice to a considerable height. The Clowds near the horizon were of a perfect Snow white-ness and were difficult to be distinguished from the Ice hills whose lofty summits reached the Clowds. The outer or Nothern edge of this immence Ice field was compose[d] of loose or broken ice so close packed together that nothing could enter it; about a Mile in began the firm ice, in one compact solid boddy and seemed to increase in height as you traced it to the South; In this field we counted Ninety Seven Ice Hills or Mountains, many of them vastly large. Such Ice Mountains as these are never seen in Greenland, so that we cannot draw a comparison between the Green-land Ice and this now before us. Was it not for the

Greenland Ships fishing yearly among such Ice (the ice hills excepted) I should not have hisitated one moment in declaring it as my opinion that the Ice we now see extended in a solid body quite to the Pole, and that it is here, i.e. to the South of this parallel, where the many Ice Islands we find floating about in the Sea are first form'd, and afterwards broke off by gales of wind and other causes, be this as it may, we must allow that these numberless and large Ice Hills must add such weight to the Ice feilds, to which they are fixed, as must make a wide difference between the Navigating this Icy Sea and that of Greenland: I will not say it was impossible anywhere to get in among this Ice, but I will assert that the bare attempting of it would be a very dangerous enterprise and what I believe no man in my situation would have thought of. I whose ambition leads me not only farther than any other man has been before me, but as far as I think it possible for man to go, was not sorry at meeting with this interruption, as it in some measure relieved us from the dangers and hardships, inseparable with the Navigation of the Southern Polar regions. Sence therefore we could not proceed one Inch farther South, no other reason need be assigned for our Tacking and stretching back to the North, being at that time in the Latitude of 71°10' South, Longitude 106°54' w. We had not be[en] long tacked before we were involved in a very thick fog, so that we thought our selves very fortunate in having clear weather when we approach'd the ice. I must observe that we saw here very few Birds of any kind; some Penguins were heard but none seen, nor any other signs of land whatever.

MONDAY 31*st*. *Therm.r. at Noon* 34. *Winds ESE to ENE. Course NBE. Dist. Sailed* 96 *Miles. Lat. in South* 69°13'. *Longd. in W. Reckg.* 105°39'. Fresh breezes and thick foggy weather with Showers of Snow, piercing cold air; the Snow and Moistness of the fog gave a Coat of Ice to our riging of near an Inch thick. Towards noon had intervals of tolerable clear weather.

[. . .]

[February 1774]

SUNDAY 6*th*. At 1 pm took the second reef in the Top-sails and got down Top g^t yards which was no sooner done than it fell Calm and soon after had variable breezes between the NW and East, attended with Snow and Sleet. In the AM we got the wind from the South, loosed all the reefs out, got top-g^t yards and set the Sails and steered North-Easterly, with a resolution to proceed directly to the North as there was no probability of finding Land in these high Latitudes, at least not on this side Cape Horn and I thought it equally as improbable any should be found on the other side, but supposing the Land laid down in Mr Dalrymples Chart to exist or that of Bouvets, before we could reach either the one or the other the Season would be too far spent to explore it this Summer, and obliged us either to have wintered upon it, or retired to Falkland Isles or the Cape of Good Hope, which ever had been done, Six or Seven Months must have been spent without being able in that time to make any discovery what ever, but if we had met with no land or other impediment we must have reached the last of these places by April at farthest when the expedition would have been finished so far as it related to the finding a Southern Continent, mentioned by all authors who have written on this subject whose assertions and conjectures are now intirely refuted as all there enquiries were confined to this Southern Pacific Ocean in which altho' there lies no continent there is however room for very large Islands, and many of those formerly discover'd within the Southern Tropick are very imperfectly explored and there situations as imperfectly known. All these things considered, and more especially as I had a good Ship, a healthy crew and no want of Stores or Provisions I thought I cou'd not do better than to spend the insuing Winter within the Tropicks: I must own I have little expectation of makeing any valuable discovery, nevertheless it must be allowed that the Sciences will receive some improvement there from especially Navigation and Geography. I had several times communicated my thoughts on this subject to Captain Furneaux, at first he seem'd not to approve of it, but was inclinable to get to the Cape of Good Hope, afterwards he seem'd to come into my opinion; I however could not well give any Instructions about it, as at that time it depended on so many circumstances and therefore cannot even guess how Captain Furneaux will act; be this as it will, my intintion is now to go in search of the Land said to be discovered by Juan Fernandas in the Latitude of 38°s, not finding any such Land, to look for Easter Island, the situation of which is so variously laid down that I have little hopes of finding [it]. I next intend to get within the Tropicks and proceed to the west on a rout differing from former Navigators, touching at, and settling the Situation of such Isles as we may meet with, and if I have time, to proceed in this manner as far west as Quiros's Land or what M. de Bougainville calls the Great Cyclades.² Quiros describes this Land, which he calls Tierra Austral del Espiritu Santo, as being very large, M. de Bougainville neither confirms nor refutes this account. I think it a point well worth clearing up; from these isles my design is to get to the South and proceed back to the East between the Latitudes of 50° and 60°, designing if Possible to be the Length of Cape Horn in November next, when we shall have the best part of the Summer before us to explore the Southern part of the Atlantick Ocean. This I must own is a great undertaking and perhaps more than I shall be able to perform as various impediments may—

[...]

[*Cook continued on a northerly course for the rest of the month and into the beginning of March. He crossed the track of the* Endeavour *(1769) and of the* Dolphin *(Walls,*

² The New Hebrides, discovered by Quirós in 1606 and redis-covered by Bougainville in 1768.

1767). There was constant observation of possible indications of land – the swell, currents, birds, driftwood, weeds – but Cook was sceptical about 'the discovery of Juan Fernandez', which was not the real island known by his name but an imaginary discovery of his seemingly invented by Juan Luis Arias and enthusiastically adopted by Dalrymple as evidence of the great southern continent. What Cook does not mention is that he fell ill about 23 February. In a later version of the journal he wrote: 'I was now taken ill of the Billious colick and so Violent as to confine me to my bed, so that the Management of the Ship was left to Mr Cooper my first Officer who conducted her very much to my satisfaction.']

[March 1774]

TUESDAY 8*th*. [*Therm.*] 75½. [*Winds*] *Easterly.* [*Course*] *N* 52° *W.* [*Dist.*] 124 *Miles.* [*Lat.*] 27° 4'. [*Long. by reckoning*] 103° 58'. [*Long. by watch*] 105° 3'. Gentle gales and fine pleasent weather. In the AM saw many Birds, such as Tropick, Men of War and Egg Birds of two sorts, grey and White, many sheer-waters or Petrels of two or three sorts, one sort small and almost all black, another sort much larger with dark grey backs and white bellies. Swell not much and from the East.

WEDNESDAY 9*th*. [*Winds*] *Easterly.* [*Course*] *W* 2° *S.* [*Dist.*] 106 *Miles.* [*Lat.*] 27° 7'. [*Long.*] 106° 00'. Weather and winds as yesterday. Judgeing our selves by observation to be nearly in the Latitude of Davis's land or

Easter Island we steer'd nearly due west meeting with the same sort of Birds as yesterday.

THURSDAY 10*th*. [*Therm.*] 76¾. [*Winds*] *Easterly.* [*Course*] *West, Southly.* [*Dist.*] 102 *Miles.* [*Lat.*] 27°9'. [*Long.*] 107°55'. In the evening took in the Studding Sails and ran under an easy sail during night, at daylight made all sail again, meeting with the same sort of Birds as yesterday and abundance of Albacores & flying fish not one of which we could catch.

FRIDAY 11*th*. [*Therm.*] 75. [*Winds*] *Easterly.* [*Course*] *W 2° S.* [*Dist.*] 60 *Miles.* [*Lat.*] 27°11'. [*Long.*] 109°2'. Gentle breeze and pleasent weather. At Midddnight brought to till day-light then made sail and soon after saw the Land from the Mast head bearing West. At Noon it was seen from the deck extending from w¾n to wbs. Distant about 12 Leagues.

SATURDAY 12*th*. At 7 o'Clock in the PM being about 5 Leagues from the island which extending from N 62° w to N 87° w we sounded but had no ground with a line of 140 fathoms; we now Shortned Sail and Stood off SE & SSE having but very little wind and at 2 AM it fell quite calm, and continued so till 10 AM when a breeze sprung up at SW & WSW with which we stood in for the land the extremes of which at Noon bore from NW to west by North distant 4 or 5 Leagues. Lat ob^d 27° South.

SUNDAY 13*th*. In stretching in for the land we discovered people and those Moniments or Idols mentioned by the Authors of Roggeweins Voyage which left us no room to doubt but it was Easter Island. At 4 o'Clock we were within about half a League of the NE point, bearing NNW where we found 35 fathom a dark sandy bottom. We plyed to windward in order to get into a Bay which appeared on the SE side of the isle, but night put a stop to our endeavours, which we spent makeing short boards, Soundings from 75 to 110 fathoms, bottom dark Sand. During night the wind was variable, but in the morning it fixed at SE, blew in squals attended with rain which ceased as the day advanced. The wind now blowing right on the SE shore on which the Sea broke very high and there being no bay or Harbour as we had immag[in]ed, I steer'd round the South point of the Island in order to explore the western side, accordingly we ran along the western and NW side at the distance of one mile from the Shore, until we open'd the nothern point without seeing any safe anchoring place. The Natives were collicted together in several places on the shore in small companies of 10 or 12. The most likely anchoring place we had seen was on the West side of the isle miles to the northward of the South point before a small sandy beach where we found 40 and 30 fathoms one mile from the Shore, Bottom dark sand, here a Canoe conducted by two Men came off and brought us a Bunch of Plantans and then returned ashore. Seeing no better anchorage than the one just mentioned we Tacked and Plyed back to the South in order to gain it.

MONDAY 14*th*. At half past 6 o'Clock PM Anchored at the place before mentioned in 36 fathom Water, the bottom a fine dark sand. Having sent the boat in shore to sound one of the natives swam off to her, came on board and remained with us all night and next day, this confidence gave us a favourable Idea of the rest of the Natives. At 3 AM a breeze from the land drove us of the bank, which after the Anchor was up we plyed in for again and in the mean time I went ashore to inform my self if any refreshments or Water were to be got. We landed at the sandy beach where about 100 of the Natives were collected who gave us no disturbance at landing, on the contrary hardly one had so much as a stick in their hands. After distributing among them some Medals and other trifles, they brought us sweet Potatoes, Plantains and some Sugar cane which they exchanged for Nails &c[a]; after having found a small Spring or rather Well made by the Natives, of very brackish Water, I returned on board and anchored the Ship in 32 f[m] Water, the bottom a fine dark sand, something more than a mile from the Shore.

TUESDAY 15*th*. PM Got on board a few Casks of Water and Traded with the Natives for some of the produce of the island which appeared in no great plenty and the Water so bad as not to be worth carrying on board, and the Ship not in safety determined me to shorten my stay here. Accordingly I sent Lieutenants Pickersgill and Edgcumb with a party of Men, accompanied by M[r] Forster and several more of the gentlemen, to examine the Country; I was not sufficiently recovered from a fit of illness to make one of the party. At the Ship employed geting on Board Water and tradeing with the Natives.

WEDNESDAY 16*th*. About 7 in the evening the exploaring party returned and the next morning Mr Pickersgill made me the following report . . .

[*Pickersgill's 'Remarks' dwelt on the barrenness of the island and the poor quality of the scanty water. They were led round the island by a man with a white flag. The great stone images they understood to be of* ariki *or chiefs; many of the images had collapsed. They had a ceremonial meeting with an imposing person whom they understood to be 'the areeke of the Island . . . called Wy-hu'. When one of the islanders caught up a bag which a member of the party had put on the ground, the trigger-happy marine officer Edgecumbe fired at him with small shot; there was a commotion but no apparent consequences.*]

This report of Mr Pickersgills so far as it regarded the Produce of the Island was confirmed by the whole party and determined me to quit the island without further delay, a breeze of wind about 10 o'Clock Coming in from Sea, attended with heavy showers of rain made this the more necessary, accordingly we got under sail and stood out to Sea, but as we had but little wind I sent a boat a shore to purchase such refreshments as the Natives might have brought to the Water side.

THURSDAY 17*th*. PM Playing off the Island with variable light winds and had a boat and people on Shore tradeing, in the evening they return'd on board when we hoisted the boat in and made Sail NW with the wind at NNE. At Noon the body of the Island bore ESE½s distant 15 Leagues. Lat Ob^d 26° 48' s.

This is undoubtedly the same Island as was seen by Roggewein in Ap^l 1722 altho' the descriptions given of it by the authors of that voyage do's by no means correspond with it now; it may also be the same as was seen by Captain Davis in 1686, but this is not altogether so certain, and if it is not then his discovery cannot lie far from the continent of America, for this Latitude seems to have been very well explored between the Meridian of 80 and 110, Captain Carteret carries it much farther, but his Track seems to be a little too far to the South . . . No Nation will ever contend for the honour of the discovery of Easter Island as there is hardly an Island in this sea which affords less refreshments and conveniences for Shiping than it does; Nature has hardly provided it with any thing fit for man to eat or drink, and as the Natives are but few and may be supposed to plant no more than sufficient for themselves, they cannot have much to spare to new comers . . .

The Inhabitants of this isle from what we have been able to see of them do not exceed six or seven hundred souls and above two thirds of these are Men, they either have but few Women among them or else many were not suffer'd to make their appearence, the latter seems most Probable. They are certainly of the same race of People as the New Zealanders and the other islanders, the affinity of the Language, Colour and some of their customs all tend to prove it, I think they bear more affinity to the Inhabitants of Amsterdam and New Zealand, than those of the more northern isles which makes it probable that there lies a chain of isles in about this Parallel or under, some of which have at different times been seen . . .

Of their Religion, Government &c^a we can say nothing with certainty. The Stupendous stone statues errected in different places along the Coast are certainly no representation of any Deity or places of worship; but most probable Burial Places for certain Tribes or Families. I myself saw a human Skeleton lying in the foundation of one just covered with Stones, what I call the foundation is an oblong square about 20 or 30 feet by 10 or 12 built of and faced with hewn stones of a vast size, executed in so masterly a manner as sufficiently shews the ingenuity of the age in which they were built. They are not all of equal height, some are not raised above two or three feet, others much more, and seems to depend on the nature of the ground on which they are built. The Statue is errected in the middle of its foundation, it is about [15 to 30 feet] high and [from 16 to 24] round for this is its shape, all the appearences it has of a human figure is in the head where all the parts are in proportion to its Size; the head is crow[n]ed with a Stone of the shape and full size of a drum, we could not help wondering how they were set up, indeed if the Island was once Inhabited by a race of Giants of 12 feet high as one of the Authors of Roggewein's Voyage tell us, then this wonder ceaseth and gives place to another equally as extraordinary, viz. to know what is become of this race of giants. Besides these Statues which are very numerous and no were but a long the Sea Coast there are many little heaps of stones here and there on the bank along the Sea Coast, two or three of the uppermost stones of these piles are generally white, perhaps always so when the pile is compleat: it can hardly be doubted but these piles of stones have some meaning tho' we do not know it.

From the report of Mr Pickersgill it should seem that the Island is under the government of one Man whom they stile Arreeke, that is King or Chief.

Some pieces of Carving were found a mongest these people which were neither ill designed nor executed. They have no other tools than what are made of Stone, Bone, Shells &c^a. They set but little value on Iron and yet they knew the use of it, perhaps they obtained their knowlidge of this Metal from the Spaniards who Viseted this Isle in 1769 some Vistiges of which still remained amongest them, such as pieces of Cloth &c^a.

[...]

[*For three weeks Cook followed a north-westerly and then a westerly course. On 6 April he calculated his position as latitude 9 °20' s, 138° 1' w.*]

[April 1774]

THURSDAY 7*th*. At 4 o'Clock in the PM after runing 4 Leagues West sence Noon, Land was seen bearing WBS distant about 9 Leagues, two hours after saw a nother land bearing SWBS and appeared more extensive than the first: hauld up for this land and kept under an easy Sail all night having Squally unsittled weather with rain. At 6 AM the Land first seen bore NW the other SW½W and a third West, I directed my Course for the Channell between these two last lands, under all the Sail we could set, having unsittled Squally Showery weather. Soon after we discovered a fourth land still more to the westward and were now well assured that these were the Marquesas discovered by Mendana in 1595. At Noon we were in the Channell which divides St Pedro and La dominica.

FRIDAY 8*th*. Continued to rainge a long the SE Shore of La Dominica without seeing any signs of an Anchoring place, till we came to the Channell which divides it from St Christina through which we pass'd and haul'd over to the last mentioned Island and ran along the shore to the South westward in search of Mendana['s] Port. After passing Several Coves in which seem'd to be tollerable Anchorage, but a great Surff on the Shore; from some of these places came of some of the Natives in their Canoes, but as we had a fresh of wind and did not shorten Sail none came up with us. At length we came to the Port we were in search after, into which we hauled and made an attempt to turn in, in the doing of which we were attacked by such Violent Squalls from the high lands that we were within a few yards of being driven against the rocks to Leeward. After escaping this danger we stood out again made a stretch to windward and then stretched in and Anchored in the Entrance of the Bay in 34 fathom water, sandy bottom, without so much as attempting to turn farther in . . . We had no soon anchored then about 30 or 40 of the Natives came round us in a Doz^n or fourteen Canoes, but it requir'd some address to get them along side, at last a Hatchet and some large Nails induced the people in one Canoe to put under the quarter gallery, after this all the others put along side and exchanged Bread fruit and some fish for small Nails and then retired a shore. But came off again to us very early the next morning in much greater numbers bringing off Bread fruit, Plantains and one Pig which they exchanged for Nails &c^a but in this Traffick they would frequently keep our goods and make no return, tell at last I was obliged to fire a Musquet ball Close past one man who had served us in this manner after which they observed a little more honisty and at length several of them came on board. At this time we were prepairing to warp the Ship farther into the Bay and I was going in a Boat to look for the most convenient place to mo[o]r her in; observing so many of the Natives on board, I said to the officers, you must look well after these people or they certainly will carry off some thing or other, these words were no sooner out of my mouth and had hardly got into my Boat, when

I was told they had stolen one of the Iron Sta[n]chions from the opposite Gang-way, I told the officers to fire over the Canoe till I could get round in the Boat, unluckily for the theif they took better aim than I ever intend and killed him the third Shott, two others that were in the same Canoe jumped overboard but got in again just as I got to the Canoe, the one was a Man and seem'd to laugh at what had happen'd, the other was a youth about 14 or 15 years of age, he looked at the dead man with a serias and dejected countinance and we had after wards reason to believe that he was son to the disceas'd. This accident made all the Canoes retire from us with precipitation. I followed them into the Bay and prevaild upon the people in one Canoe to come along side the Boat and receive some Nails and other things I gave them. When I returned on board we carried out a Kedge Anchor with 3 hawsers upon an end to warp in by the hove short on the bower. One would have thought that the Natives by this time were fully sencible of the effect of our fire Arms but the event proved other wise for the boat had no sooner left the Kedge anchor than a Canoe put of from the Shore, took hold of the Buoy and attempted, as we supposed, to drag what was fast to the rope a shore, but fearing they would at last take away the Buoy I ordered a Musquet to be fire[d] at them, but as the ball fell short they took no notice of it, but the 2nd ball that was fired pass'd over them on which they let go the buoy and made for the shore and this was the last shott we had occasion to fire and probably had more effect upon them than killing the Man as it shewed them that they were hardly safe at any distance for they afterwards stood in great dread of the Musquet, nevertheless they would very often exercize their tallant of thieving upon us, which I thought necessary to put up with as our stay was likely to be but short among them. The Natives had retarded us so long that before we were ready to heave up the anchor and warp in the wind began to blow in Squalls out of the Bay, so that we were obliged to lay fast where we were.

It was not long before the Natives ventured off to us again, in the first Canoe which came was a man who seem'd of some consequence, he advanced slowly with a Pig upon his Shoulder which he sold for a Spike nail as soon as he got a long side. I made him a present of a Hatchet and several other Articles which induced him to come into the Ship where he made a short stay and then retired; his example was followed by all the other Canoes and trade was presently reestablished. Things being thus Settled on board I went a shore with a party of Men to try what was to be done there, we were received by the Natives as if nothing had happened, traded with them for some Plantains and a few Sm^l Piggs and after Loading the Launch with water returned on board to dinner.

SATURDAY 9*th*. PM sent the boats and a guard a Shore again for Water; upon their landing the Natives all fleed but one Man and he seemed much frightned, he was disir'd to go and fetch some fruit which he did accordingly and after him one or two more came and these were all that were seen till 8 o'Clock in the AM at which time some made their appearance just as the Boats put off from the Watering place; after breakfast I went a Shore my self before the guard when the Natives crowded round me in great numbers but as soon as the guard landed I had enough to do to prevent them from runing off, at length their fears were dissipated and a trade opened for fruit and Pigs. I believe the reason of their flying from our people last evening was their not seeing me at the head of them, for they certainly would have done the same now had I not been present. Towards Noon a chief of some consequence, attended by a great number of People, came down to us, I made him a present of Nails and Several other Articles and in return he gave me some of his ornaments, after these Mutal exchanges a good under Standing Seemed to be settled between us and them so that we got by exchanges as much fruit as Loaded two boats and then return on board.

SUNDAY 10*th*. PM Launch Watering and a party Trading with the Natives, went my self into the Southern cove of the Bay where I procured five Pigs, and came to the House which we were told belonged to the Man we had kill'd; there were Six Piggs in it which we were told belonged to the deceased Son who had fled upon our approach. I wanted much to have seen him to have made him a present and by other kind treatment convinced him and the others that it was not from any bad design we had against the Nation we had kill'd his father; it would have been to no purpose my leaving any thing in the house as it certainly would have been taken away by others. Strict honisty was seldom observed amongst them selves when the property of our things came to be disputed, I saw a Striking instance of this. I offered a man a Six Inch Spike for a Pig which he readily excepted of and hand'd the pig to a nother man to give me which was done and the Spike given in return, but in stead of giving it to the Man who sold the Pig he kept it him self and offered him in lieu a Sixpenny Nail, words of course arose and I waited to see how it would end, but as the man who had got posession of the Spike seem'd resolved to keep it I left them before it was desided.

AM Em^pd as usual (viz) in Watering and Trading with the Natives. Some Canoes from more distant parts came and sold us some Pigs so that we had now sufficient to give all hands a fresh meal, the Pigs they bring us are so small that 40 or 50 are hardly sufficient for this purpose.

MONDAY 11*th*. In the PM I made an expedition towards Southward in which I collected 18 Pigs and I believe should have got more had I had more time, in the Morning I went to the same places but instead of geting Pigs as I expected I found every thing quite changed, the Nails and other things they were Mad after the Evening before they now dispised and in stead of them they wanted they did not know what, the reason of this was, some of the young gentlemen having been a Shore the preceeding day and had given them in exchange various Articles such as they had not seen before and which took with them more than Nails, or perhaps they thought they had already enough of these and wanted some thing more curious, which I nor indeed any one else had to give them sufficient to supply us with refreshments, thus our market was at once spoil'd and I was obliged to return with 3 or 4 little Pigs which cost me more than a Doz^n would have done the evening before; when I got on board I found that the party at the water place had had no better success. When I saw that this place was not likely to supply us with sufficient refreshments, not very convenient for geting off wood and Water nor for giving the Ship the necessary repairs, I resolv'd forth with to leave it and seack for some place that would supply our wants better, for it must be supposed that after having been 19 Weeks at Sea (for I cannot call the two or 3 days spent at Easter Island any thing else) living all the time upon a Salt Diet, but what we must want some refreshments altho I must own and that with pleasure, that on our arrival here, it could hardly be said that we had one Sick Man on board and not above two or three who had the least complaint, this was undoubtedly owing to the many antiscorbutic articles we had on board and the great care and Attention of the Surgeon who took special care to apply them in time.

TUESDAY 12*th*. At 3 o'Clock in the PM weighed and Stood over for St Dominica in order to take a View of the West side of that Island but as we could not reach it before dark the night was spent Plying between the two Islands. In the morning we had a full View of the SW and western sides of the Isle neither of which seem'd to afford any Anchorage. At 8 o'Clock we were off the NW point from which the land trended NE Easterly, so that this side was not likely to have any safe Port as being exposed to the Easterly winds; we had now but little and that very variable with Showers of Rain: at length we got a breeze at ENE with which we steered to the South ward with a view of leaving these Isles altogether . . .

WEDNESDAY 13*th*. *Winds NE to ESE. Course S 36° West. Distce Sailed 75 Miles. Latde in* 10°56'. *Longde in West* 139°54'. Gentle breezes with rain. At 5 o'Clock in the PM the Harbour of Madre de Dios bore ENE½E distant 5 Leagues and the body of the Island Magdalena SE about 9 Leagues; this was the only View we had of this last isle. From hence I directed my Course SSW½W for Otaheite and likewise with a view of falling in with Some of those isles discovered by former Navigators whose Situations are not well determined.

[. . .]

[*Cook made a brief stop at Takaroa in the Tuamotu archipelago, where he had an uncertain reception. As they left, Cook 'ordered two or three Guns to be fired over the little isle the Natives were upon in order to shew them that it was not their own Superior strength and Numbers which obliged us to leave their isle'.*]

THURSDAY 21*st*. *Winds EBN. Course S* 38°45'. *Dist. Sailed* 113 *M. Lat. in* 17°32'. *Longde. in* 148°42'. First part fresh gales with rain, remainder fair and Clowdy. At

10 AM Saw the high land of Otaheite and at Noon Point Venus bore west-northerly distant 13 Leagues.

FRIDAY 22nd. *Winds Easterly. Lat. in* 17°29'. *Longde. in* 149°35', *[watch]* 151°44'. PM Moderate breezes and Clowdy. At 7 Shortned Sail and spent the night plying of and on. AM Squally with heavy Showers of rain. At 8 Anchored in Matavai Bay in 7 fathom Water, which was no sooner done than we were viseted by several of our old friends, who express'd not a little joy at seeing us.

As my reasons for puting in here was to give Mr Wales an oppertunity to know the error of the Watch from the known Longitude of this place and to determine a fresh her rate of going; the first thing we did was to land his Instruments &c^a and to set up tents for the reception of a guard and such others as it was necessary to have on Shore. As to Sick we had none.

SATURDAY 23rd. *Showery rainy Weather.* The Natives begin to bring us in refreshments, such as fruit and Fish, sufficient for all hands.

SUNDAY 24th. *Otou* the King with a vast train and several Chiefs of distinction paid us a Viset and brought with them as presents Ten or a Doz^n Hogs which made them exceeding welcome. I was advertised of the Kings coming and met him at the Tents a shore, conducted him on board where he stay'd Dinner, after which he and his attendance were dismiss'd with Suteable presents.

MONDAY 25*th*. Much rain, Thunder and Lightning. Nevertheless I had a nother Viset from Otou who brought with him a quantity of refreshments &c[a]. When we were at Amsterdam, among other Curosities we Collected some red Parrot Feathers which were highly Valued by these people; When this came to be known in the isle all the Principal people of both Sex endeavour'd by every means in their power to Ingratiate themselves into our favour in order to obtain these Valuable Jewels by bring[ing] us Hogs and every other thing the Island produced, and generally for Tiyo (Friendship) but they always took care to let us know that Oora (red Feathers) were to be a part of the return we were to make. Having these Feathers was a very fortunate circumstance to us for as they were Valuable to the Natives they became so to us allso, for our Stock of trade was by this time greatly exhausted and if it had not been for them I should have found it difficult to have supplyed the Ships with the necessary refreshments.

When I put in here my intention was to stay but a few days, that is no longer than M[r] Wales had made the Obser[ns] for the purpose already mentioned from a supposition founded on the reception we met with the last time we were here that we should get no Hogs; but the Number the Natives have already brought us and the few excursions we have made which have not exceeded the Plains of Matavai and Oparre hath convinced us of our error. We find at these two places built and building a great number of Canoes and houses both large and small, People living in spacious houses who had not a place to shelter themselves in Eight Months ago, several large hogs near every house and every other Sign of a riseing state.

Judging from these favourable circumstances that we should not mend our Situation by removeing to a nother island I therefore resolved to make a longer stay & to begin with the repairs of the Ship; accordingly I ordered the empty Casks and Sails to be got on shore to repair, the Smiths Forge to be set up to repair our Iron work, the Ship to be Caulked and the rigging &c^a to be overhauled, Works which the high Southern Latitudes had made highly necessary.

TUESDAY 26*th*. In the Morning I set out for Oparre accompaned by the two Mr Forsters and some of the officers to pay Otou a formal Viset by appointment, as we approached Oparre we observed a number of large Canoes in Motion; but we were surprised when we got there to see upwards of three-hundred of them all rainged in good order for some distance along the Shore all Compleatly equip'd and Man'd, and a vast Crowd of Men on the Shore; So unexpected an Armament collected together in our Neighbourhood in the space of one night gave rise to various conjectures: we landed however and were received by a Vast Multitude some under Arms and some not the cry of the latter was Tiyo no Otou and the former Tiyo no Towha, this Cheif as we soon after learnt was General or Admiral of the fleet. I was met by him presently after we landed, he received me with great Courtesy and then took hold of my right hand. A Chief whose name was Tee, Uncle to the King and one of his Prime Ministers, had hold of my left, thus I was draged along as it were between two parties, both declaring themselves our friends, the one wanted me to stay by the fleet and the other to go to the King, at last coming to the general place of Audience a Mat was spread on the ground for me to sit down upon and Tee went to bring the King, Towha was unwilling I should sit down but partly insisted on my going to the fleet but as I knew nothing of this Chief I did not comply; presently Tee return'd and wanted to conduct me to the King and took me by the hand for that purpose, this Towha opposed so that between the one party and the other I was like to have been torn to pieces and was obliged to disire Tee to desist, and to go with the Admiral and his party to the fleet. As soon as we came before the Admirals Vessel two lines of Arm'd Men were drawn up on the shore before her to keep of the Crowd and clear the way for me to go in, but as I was determined not to go (unless forced) I made the Water which was between me and the Canoe an excuse, this did not answer for a Man immidiately squated himself down at my feet and offered to carry me in and then I declar'd I would not go and that very moment Towha quited me without my seeing which way he went nor would any one inform me; I therefore turn'd back and inquired for the King, Tee who I believe never lost sight of me, came and told me he was gone into the Country Mataou and advised me to go to my boat which we according did as soon as we got all together for Mr Edgcumb was the only gentleman that could keep with me, the others were jostled about in the crowd in the same Manner as we were. When we had got into our boat we took our time to view this fleet, the Vessels of War consisted of 160 large double Canoes, very well equip'd, Man'd and Arm'd, altho' I am not sure that they had on board either their full compliment of Fighting men or rowers, I rather think not. The Cheifs ie all those on the Fighting Stages were drist in their War habits, that is in a vast quantity of Cloth Turbands, breast Plates and Helmmets, some of the latter are of such a length as to greatly incumber the wearer, indeed their whole dress seem'd ill calculated for the day of Battle and seems to be design'd more for shew than use, be this as it may they certainly added grandure to the Prospect, as they were complesant enough to Shew themselves to the best advantage, their Vessels were decorated with Flags, Streamers &c^a so that the whole made a grand and Noble appearence such as was never seen before in this Sea, their implements of war were Clubs, pikes and Stones. These Canoes were rainged close along side each other with their heads a Shore and Sterns to the Sea, the Admirals Vesel was, as near as I could guess, in the center. Besides these Vesels of War there were 170 Sail of Smaller double Canoes, all with a little house upon them and rigg'd with Masts and sails which the others had not; These Canoes must be design'd for Transporte or Victulars or both and to receive the wounded Men &c^a; in the War Canoes were no sort of Provisions whatever. In these 330 Canoes I judged there were no less than 7760 Men a number which appears incredible, especially as we were told that they all belonged to the districts of Attahourou and Ahopatea . . .

When we had well view'd this fleet I wanted much to see the Admiral to have gone with him on board the Vesels, I enquired for him as we rowed past the Vesels to no purpose, we then put a shore and inquire'd for him, but the noise and Crowd was so great that no one attended to what we said, at last Tee came and whispered us in the ear that the King was gone to Matavai and advised us to go their also and not to land where we were, we took his advice put off and row'd for the Ship accordingly, this account and advice of Tee gave rise to new conjectures, in short we conclude that this Towha was some disaffected Chief upon the point of making War against his King. We had not long left Oparre before the whole fleet was in Motion and proceeded back to the westward from whence they came.

When we got on board the Ship, we were told that this fleet was a part of the armament intended to go against Eimeo whose Chief had revolted from Otou his Lawfull Sovereign. I was also inform'd that Otou was not nor had been at Matavai, and therefore after dinner I went again to Oparre where I found him, I now learn that his fears and the reason of his not seeing us in the Morning was occasioned by some of his people stealing (owing to the neglect of the washerman) a quantity of my Clothes and was fearfull least I should demand restitution, when I assured him I should not disturb the peace of the isle on any such occasion he was satisfied; I likewise understood that Towha was alarm'd partly on this account and partly by my not honoring him with my company on board his fleet when he desired it. I was Jealous at seeing such a Force in our neigherhood without being able to know any thing of its design; thus by misunderstanding one a nother I lost the oppertunity of examining more narrowly into a part of the Naval force of this Island and makeing my self better acquainted how it acts and is conducted. Such a nother oppertunity may never happen again as it was commanded by a brave, Sencible and intelligent Chief who no doubt would have satisfied us in all the questions we had thought proper to ask and as the Objects were before our eyes we could not well have mistook one another. Matter[s] being Thus cleared up and mutual presents having pass'd between Otou and me we return'd on board in the evening.

WEDNESDAY 27th. Morning, Received a present from Towha consisting of Two Large hogs and some fruit sent me by two of his Servants who had orders to receive nothing in return. Soon after I took a trip in my boat to Oparre were I found both this chief and the King, after a Short Stay I brought them both on board to dinner together with the Kings Brother, they were shew'd all over the Ship, the Admiral who had never seen such a one before view'd every thing with great attention and express'd much surprise at what he saw. After dinner he put a Hog on board the Ship and retired before I had time to make him any return either for this or what I had in the Morning and soon after the King and his Brother took leave. The King seem'd not only to pay the Admiral much respect himself but was desireous I should do the same, he was nevertheless certainly jelous of him, but on what account we knew not for it was but the day before he frankly told us the Admiral was not his friend. Both these Chiefs when on board to day Solicited me to assist them against the people of Tiarabou altho at this time the two Kin[g]doms are at peace and we were told go with their joint force against Eimeo. To this request of theirs I made an evasive answer which I believe they understood was not favourable to their request.

THURSDAY 28*th*. Remaind on board all day. Had a Present of a Hog sent me by Oheatua the King of Tiarabou, for which in return he disired a few red feathers. In the afternoon Mr Forster and his party set out for the Mountains with an intent to Stay out the night.

FRIDAY 29*th*. Early in the Morn Otou, Towha and Several other Grandees came on board and brought with them not only provisions but some of the Most Valuable curiosities in the island which they gave to me and for which I made them such returns as they were well pleased with, I likewise took the opportunity to repay the civilties I had received from Towha.

Last night one of the Natives made an Attempt to Steal one of our Water Casks from the Watering Place, he was caught, sent on board and put in Irons in which Situation he was found by the two Chiefs to whom I made known his crime. Otou beg'd he might be set at liberty which I refused tilling him it was but Just the

Man should be punished, accordingly I ordered him a
shore to the Tent, where I went my self with the two
Chiefs and others, here I ordered the Man to be tyed
up to a Post, Otou his Sister and some others beg'd
hard for the Man, Towha said not one word but was
very attentive to every thing going forward; I expostu-
lated with Otou on the conduct of this Man and his
people in general tilling him that neither I nor any of
my people took any thing from him or his people
without first paying for it and innumirated the Articles
we gave for such and such things and that he well knew
that when any of my people broke through these rules
they were punished for it and that it was but right this
man should be punished also, besides I told him it
would be the means of saving the lives of some of his
people by detering them from commiting crimes of
this nature in which some would be kill'd at one time
or a nother; I said more to the same purpose most of
which I believe he pretty well understood as he was
satisfied and only desired the Man might not be kill'd.
I then ordered the guard out to keep the Crowd which
was very great at a proper distance and in Sight of
them all ordered the fellow two dozen lashes with a
Cat of Nine tails which he bore with great firmness,
he was then set at liberty and Towha the Admiral
began to Harangue the crowd for not a man left us on
this occasion, he spoke for a full quarter of an hour and
with seemingly great Perspicuity and he was heard with
great Attention, his speach consisted mostly of short
Sentences, nevertheless I could understand but few
words, he recapitulated most of what I had said to

Otou, named several Advantages they had received from us, condemn'd their present conduct and recommended a different one for the future. Otou on this occasion spoke not one word. As soon as the Chief had ended his speach I order'd the Marines to go through their exercise and to Load and fire which gave the Two Chiefs, especially the Admiral, much entertainment, this done I invited them on board to dinner but they excused themselves took leave and retired with all their attendance . . .

[. . .]

[May 1774]

SATURDAY 7*th.* On going a Shore in the Morning I found Otou at the Tents and took the Oppertunity to ask his leave to cut down some trees for fuel, he not well understanding me I took him to some standing near the Shore and fit for nothing else, these he gave me leave to cut down, but as they were not Sufficient I desired he would let us know where we could get more, declaring at the same time that I should Cut down no trees which bore any fruit, he was so pleased with this declaration that he told it a loud three times to the people about us.

In the afternoon he and the whole Royal Family (Viz) his Father, Brother and three Sisters with their attendants, made me a Viset on board; His Father made me a present of a compleat Mourning dress, curiosities we most valued, in return I gave him what ever he desired and distributed red feathers to all the others and then conducted them a shore in my boat; Otou was so well pleased with the reception he and his friends had met with that he told me at parting, I might cut down as many and what Trees I pleased.

SUNDAY 8*th*. Last Night in the Middle Watch through the negligence of one of the Sentinels on Shore all our Friendly connections received an interruption, he having either slept or quited his Post gave one of the Natives an oppertunity to carry off his Musquet, the first news I heard of it was brought me in the morning by Tee whom Otou sent for this purpose and to desire I would go to him for he was Mata-ou (frightned, alarmd &c). I did not fully understand the story of the Musquit till I got on shore and was inform'd of it by the Serj^t who had the Command. I found the Natives were all alarm'd and the most of them fled, the Kings Brother slept on board all night and came a Shore with me, but having heard the whole story from Tee he gave me the Slip in a Moment before I knew well what was the matter. I cross'd the River and went alone with Tee and some others into the Woods in search of Otou. As we went a long I endeavoured to allay the fears of the People but at the same time insisted on having the Musquet return'd. After traveling some distance in the woods, enquiring of every one we met where Otou was, Tee stop'd all at once and advised me to go back for that Otou was gone towards the Mountains, that he would go to him and tell him that I was still his friend and that he would use his endeavours to have the Musquet return'd. I was satisfied by this time it was to no purpose my going farther, for altho' I was alone and without Arms, Otou's fears were such that he dar'd not see me and therefore took Tees advice and return'd. As soon as I got on board I sent Odiddy to Otou to let him know I only requird the return of the Musquet which I knew to be in his power to do . . .

[. . .]

[*The space which Cook gave to his account of the rest of this affair shows the supreme gravity not so much of the theft but of the possibility that the Tahitians would be equipped with firearms. Attempts to capture canoes and take hostages were exasperatingly frustrated. Cook was fed with information which he did not know whether to believe that the thief was from Taiarapu in the south. Suddenly and mysteriously the missing musket was returned. Cook was unable to clear up the affair because Tu, deeply upset that muskets had been fired at canoes, cut off the supplies which Cook needed. Conciliation was inevitable, and the affair ended with Cook ordering a salvo of the ship's 'great guns' to be fired at Tu's request, and a firework display.*]

WEDNESDAY 11*th*. In the Morning had a very large Supply of Fruit brought us from all parts, some of which came from Towha the Admiral, sent as usual by his Servants with orders to receive nothing in return, only desired to see me at Attahourou as he was ill and could not come to me; as I could not well undertake this Journey now I sent Odiddy along with his Servants with a present sutable to those I had in so genteel a manner received from Towha. As the Most Essential repairs of the Ship were now nearly finished I resolved to leave the isle in a few days, accordingly ordered every thing to be got off from the Shore, that the Natives might see we were about to depart.

THURSDAY 12*th*. Showery Rainy weather. To Day we had a Viset from Old Obarea the Dolphins Queen who looked as well and as young as ever. She presented me with two Hogs, some Cloth &c[a]. Presently after her came Otou with a great retinue and a great quantity of Provisions, to every one of them I made large presents thinking it might be the last time I should see them and in the evening entertain'd them with fire works.

FRIDAY 13*th*. Winds Easter, fair Weather. Two things prevented our Sailing this Morning, first Odiddy was not yet return'd from Attahourou, Secondly Otou desired I would not sail till he had seen me again; various were the reports about Odiddy, some said he was return'd, others that he was at Oparre and others said he would not return. In the evening a party of us went down to Oparre to learn more of the truth, here we found not only Odiddy, but Towha also who notwithstanding his ill state of health had resolved to see me before I went away and had got thus far on his Journey, he had got a swelling in his feet and legs which had intirely taken away the use of them; our visit was short for after seeing Otou we return'd with Odiddy on board, this youth I found was desirous of remaining at this isle and therefore told him he was at liberty to remain here or at Ulietea and Frankly told him that if he went to England it was highly probable he would never return, but if after all he choosed to go I would take care of him and he must look upon me as his Father, he threw his arms about me and wept saying many people persuaded him to stay at the isle. I told him to go a Shore and speak with his friends and then come to me in the morning. He was very well beloved in the Ship for which reason every one was persuading him to go with us, telling what great things he wou'd see and return with immence riches, according to his Idea of riches, but I thought proper to undeceive him, thinking it an Act of the highest injustice to take away a person from these isles against his own free inclination under any promise whatever much more that of bringing them back again, what Man on board can make such a promise as this. At this time it was quite unnecessary to persuade any one to go with us, there were many youths who Voluntary offered themselves to go with us and even to remain and die in Brit-tania. The King importuned me very much to take one or two to collect red feathers for him at Amsterdam, willing to risk the chance of their returning or no; some of the gentle[men] on board were desirous of takeing some as Servants, but I refused all manner of Solicitations of this kind, knowing from experience that they would be of no use to us in the course of the Voyage, but what had the greatest weight with me was the thinking my self bound to see they were after wards properly taken care of as they could not be taken from their Native spot without my consent.

SATURDAY 14*th*. Early in the Morning Odiddy came on board with a resolution to stay at the Isle, but Mr Forster prevailed upon him to go with us to Ulietea. Soon after Towha came a long side and also several more of our friends with fruit &c^a. Towha was hoisted in and place'd in a Chair on the Quarter deck, amongest the various articles I gave this Chief was an English Pendant, told him the use of it and instructed him in what manner and where it was to be hoisted in his Canoe, after which he seem'd highly pleased. We had no sooner dispatched our friends than we saw a Number of War Canoes coming round the point of Oparre, being desirous to have a nearer view of them I hastned down to Oparre (accompanied by some of the officers &c^a) which we reached before the Canoes were all landed and had an oportunity to see in what manner they approached the shore . . . This fleet consisted of Forty sail, were equiped in the same manner as those we had seen before and belonged to the little district of Tettaha and were come to Oparre to be reviewed before Otou as those we had seen before had done . . . Otou who was present caused some of the Troops to go through their exercize on Shore, Two parties first began with Clubs, but this was so soon over that I had no time to make observations upon it, they then went to Single Combat and went thro' the

Various Mithods of fighting with great allertness and parried off the blows, pushes &c^a each combatant intended the other with great dexterity . . .

This being over the fleet depart as fast as they were got afloat and I went with Otou to one of his large double Canoes which was building and nearly ready to launch. She was by far the largest I had seen at any of the isles, he beged of me a grapling and grapling rope for her to which I aded an English Jack and Pendant, the use of which he had been before fully instructed in. I desired that these two Joint Canoes, ie what is understood as a double Canoe, might be call'd Britanne (Brit-tania) the name they have addopted for our Country, to which he very readily consented and she was Christened accordingly . . . The King came on board with us and after dinner took a Most Affectionate leave, he hardly ever ceased to day Soliciting me to return and just before he went out of the Ship took a youth by the hand, presented him to me and disired I would take him on board to Collect red feathers, I told him I could not take him knowing he would never return, but that if any Ship should happen to come here again from Brit-tania I would take care to either bring or send him plenty of red feathers; this seem'd to satisfy him, but the youth was exceedinly disireous of going and had I not made a resolution to carry no one from the isles I believe I should have taken him.

Otou remained along side of the Ship till we were under sail when he put off and we Saluted him with three guns. Our treatment at this isle was such as had induced one of our gunners mates to form a Plan to

remain at it, he knew he could not execute it with
success while we lay in the Bay, therefore took the
oppertunity as soon as we were out and all our Sails set
to slip over board (he being a good swimer) but he was
discov[er]ed before he had got clear of the Ship, we
presently Broug^t to, hoisted out a boat and sent and
took him up: a Canoe was observed about half way
between us and the Shore seemingly coming after us,
she was intended to take him in, but seeing our boat,
kept at a distance, this was a preconcerted plan between
the Man and the Natives with which Otou was
acquainted and had incouraged. I kept the Man in
confinement till we were clear of the isles then dismiss'd [him] without any other punishment, for when
I considered the situation of the Man in life I did not
think him so culpable as it may at first appear, he was
an Irishman by birth, a good Seaman and had Saild
both in the English and Dutch Service. I pick'd him
up at Batavi in my return home from my last Voyage
and he had remained with me ever sence. I never learnt
that he had either friends or connection to confine him
to any particular part of the world, all Nations were
alike to him, where than can Such a Man spend his
days better than at one of these isles where he can injoy
all the necessaries and some of the luxuries of life in
ease and Plenty. As soon as the Boat was hoisted in
again we directed our Course for Huahine in order to
pay a Viset to our friends there . . .

SUNDAY 15*th*. I have already mentioned that after leaving Otaheite we directed our Course for Huahine and

at one o'Clock in the after noon of this day Anchor'd in the North entrance of Owharre Harbour, hoisted out the boats and Warp'd into a proper birth and there Moor'd the Ship. While this was doing several of the Natives came on board amongest whom was Oree the Chief, he brought with him a Hog and some other Articles which he presented to me with the usual cerimony.

MONDAY 16*th*. In the Morning I return'd Oree's Visset and made my present in return, after which he put two Hogs into my boat and he and several of his friends came on board and dined, after dinner I gave to Oree Axes, Nails &c[a] and desired he would distribute them to his friends which he accordingly did seemingly to the satisfaction of every one.

M[r] F. and his party being out botanizing his Serv[t] a feeble Man was set upon by five or Six fellows who would have strip'd him if they had not been prevented by a nother of the party.

TUESDAY 17*th*. Being on shore in the after-noon Oree sent for me to a large house where were collected a good number of people, here a kind of Councel was hild. I well understood it regarded us and that the Chiefs all declared they had no hand in asulting M[r] F Servant and desired I would Matte[3] the fellows who did. I assured Oree that I was satisfied neither he or any of the people present had any hand in it and that

---

[3] *matte*: punish, beat (Tahitian, also used in Tonga).

I should certainly do with the fellows as they desird but the Quiry was where and how I was to find them. After this the Councel broke up.

WEDNESDAY 18*th*. Some Showers of rain. Morning Oree came with a present of fruit, stay'd dinner and in the after noon desired to see some great guns fired, Shotted, which I comply'd with and then he return'd a shore well satisfied. Some of the Petty officers going out into the Country took two men as guides and to carry their money bags, containing hatchets, Nails &c^a the Currant coin of these countries, but the fellows found means to move off with their burdthens and the Method they took was artfull enough, they pointed out to them some birds to shoot, one of the two Musquets they had went of and the other miss'd fire several times, so that they saw they were secure from both and ran off immediately and left the gentlemen gazeing at them like fools.

[. . .]

FRIDAY 20*th*. Early in the Morning three of the officers set out on a Shooting party, about 3 o'Clock in the after-noon I received intelligence that they were Seized and stripd of every thing about them, immidiately upon this I went a Shore with Mr F. and a boats crew and took possession of a large house with all the effects in it and two Chiefs, but in such a manner that they hardly knew what we were about being unwilling to alarm the neighbourhood. In this situation we were till the officers returnd safe and had had all their things restored; some insult on their side induced the Natives (who perhaps waited for such an opportunity) to seize their guns, upon which a scuffle insued, some chiefs interfeer'd and took the officers out of the Crowd and caused what had been taken from them to be restored. I wint to look for Oree to complain of those repeated outrages, but not being in the neghberhood did not see him, after I had got on board I was told he was come to his house and was much grieved at what had happend.

SATURDAY 21*st*. Early in the Morn sail'd from hence for Ulietea, upward of Sixty Canoes, we were told the people in them were Arioe's and were going to the neghbouring isles to viset their Brethren of the same ferternity, one may almost compair these Men to free masons, they tell us they assist each other when need requires and they seem to have Customs amongest them which they either will not or cannot explain, Odiddy says he is one and yet he cannot give us hardly any Idea of them.

Odiddy who generly sleeps on Shore came off with a Message from Oree desiring I would come on shore with 22 Men to go with him to Chastise the robers, the Messenger brought with him 22 pices of leaves least as I suppose he should forget his number, but this is one of their customs. Upon my receiving this extraordinary message I went ashore for better information; all I could learn from the Chief was these fellows were a sort of Banditi that had form'd themselves into a boddy with a resolution to seize and rob our people where ever they found them and therefore he wanted them chastized. I told him they would fly to the Mountains, he said no they had arm'd themselves to fight us.

When I got on board I acquainted the officers with what I had heard and desired to have their opinion of the Matter, in short it was concluded to go upon this consideration, that if we declined it as it was at the request of the chief, these fellows would thereby be incouraged to commit greater acts of Violence and as these proceeding[s] would soon reach Ulietea, at which isle we intended to touch, the people there might treat us in the same manner or worse as being more numerous. Accordingly we landed 48 Men including my self, Mr F. and officers, the Cheif join'd us with a few people and we set out on our march in good order, the Chiefs party gather'd like a snow ball as we marched thro' the Country, some arm'd and some not; Odiddy who was with us began to be alarm'd and told us that many of the people in our company were of the party we were going against and at last told us that they were only leading us to some place where they could attack us to advantage, whether there was any truth in this or only occasioned by Odiddies fears I will not pretend to say, he however was the only person we could confide in and we regulated our march accordingly; after we had march'd several miles we got intelligence that the people we were going against were fled to the Mountains, but I think we were not told this till I had diclar'd to the Chief that I would March no farther for we were then about crossing a deep Vally bounded on each side with Steep Rocks where a few men with stones only might have cut off our retreat supposeing their intention to be what Odiddy had said and what he still abided by; having therefore no business to proceed farther we return'd back in the same order as we went, and saw in several places people come down from the sides of the hills with their arms in their hands, which they laid down when ever they found they were seen by us, this shews that there must have been some truth in what Odiddy had said, but I must acquit Oree the Chief from having any hand in it. In our return Stoping at a house to refresh our selves with Cocoa-nutts two Chiefs brought each of them a pig and a dog and with the Customary ceremony presented them to me together with some young plantain trees by way of making and ratifying the Peace, after this we continued our march to the landing place where we imbarqued and went on board, soon after the chief follow'd, with a quantity of fruit and set down with us to dinner, we had scarce dined before more fruit and two Hogs were brought off to the Ship, so that we were likely to get more by this excursion than by all the presents we had made them; it certainly gave them some Alarm to see so strong a party march into the Country and probably gave them a better opinion of our fire Arms, for I had caused the people on our return to the beach to fire several vollies to let the Natives see we could keep up a constant fire for I believe they had but an indifferent or rather contemptable Idea of Musquets in general, having never seen any fired but at birds &c^a by such of our people as used to stragling about the Country, the most of them but indifferent sportsmen and Miss'd generally two Shott out of three, this together with their pieces missing fire, being Slow in charging and before the Natives, all this they no doubt took great Notice of and concluded that Musquets were not such terrible things as they had been tought to believe.

[...]

MONDAY 23rd. Winds Easterly, as it has been ever sence we have been here. The Ship being unmoor'd and every thing in readiness to Sail, at 8 AM wieghed and put to Sea, the good old Chief was the last of the Natives who went out of the Ship, when he took leave I told him we should see each other no more at which he wept saying than let your sons come we will treat them well. Oree is a good Man to the utmost sence of the word, but many of the people are far from being of that disposision and seem to take advantage of his old age. The gentle treatment they have ever met with from me and the careless and imprudent manner many of our people have rambled about in their country from a Vain opinion that fire Arms rendred them invincible hath incouraged some of these people to commit acts of Violence no man at Otaheite ever dar'd attempt.

During our stay at this isle we got bread fruit, Cocoa nuts &cᵃ more than we could well consume, but Hogs not by far sufficient for our daily expence and yet they did not appear to be scarce in the isle, it must however be Allowed that the number we took away when last here must have thin'd them much and at the same time Stock'd the Natives with our articles, besides we now wanted a proper assortment of Trade our Stock being nearly exhausted and the few Red feathers we had left was here of little Value when compared to what they bore at Otaheite, this obliged me to set the Smiths to work to make different sorts of Iron tools, Nails &c^a, in order to inable me to procure refreshments at the other isles and to support my Credit and influance among them.

MONDAY 23rd.[4] As Soon as we were clear of Hauheine we made Sail and steer'd over for the South end of Ulietea, one of the Natives of the first isle took a Passage with us as some others had done from Otaheite. Having but little wind all the afternoon it was dark by such time as we reached the West side of the isle where we spent the night. The same light and variable winds continued till 10 o'Clock ye next morning when the Trade wind at East prevail'd and we ventured to ply up to the Harbour, first sending a boat to ly in Anchorage; after makeing a few trips, anchor'd in 20 fathom water, between the two points of the reef which form the entrance on which the Sea broke with Such height and Violence as was frightfull to look at; having all our Boats and Warpes in readiness we presently carried them out and Warped the Ship in to safety where we droped an Anchor for the night. While we were warping into the harbour my old friend Oreo the Chief and Several more came off to see us. The Chief came not empty handed.

[. . .]

---

[4] Cook begins another Monday at noon as he moves from civil time to ship's time.

WEDNESDAY 25*th*. Rainy Weather, AM Warp'd the Ship up into the Cove which fronts the entrance of the Harbour and higher up than we had ever anchor'd before and there moor'd her, in this situation we commanded the Shores all round us. Whilest this was doing I went on Shore accompanied by Mr F. &c^a to make the Chief the Customary present. At our first entering his house we were met by 4 or 5 old Women, Weeping and lamenting, as it were, most bitterly and at the same time cuting their heads with Instruments made of Sharks teeth so that the blood ran p[l]entifully down their faces and on their Shoulders, and what was still worse we were obliged to submit to the Embraces of these old Hags and by that means got all besmear'd with Blood: this ceremony (for it was meerly such) being over, these women went and Washed themselves and immediately after appear'd as Cheerfull as any of the Company. After I had given my presents to the Chief and his friends he put a Hog and some fruit into my Boat and came on board with us to dinner. In the after-noon we had a vast number of Canoes and people about us from different parts of the isle, they all took up their quarters in our neighbourhood where they remain'd feasting for two or three days. We understood the most of them were Arioe's.

[...]

FRIDAY 27*th*. In the Morning Oreo, his Wife, Son and Daughters and several more of his friends came aboard and brought with them a supply of refreshments. After dinner we went on Shore and were entertained with a

Play which ended with the representation of a Woman in Labour, who at last brought forth a thumping Boy near six feet high who ran about the stage draging what was to represent the [afterbirth or umbilical cord] after him. I had an oppertunity to see this acted afterward, and observed that as soon as they got hold of the fellow who represented the child they f[l]atned his nose or press'd it to his face which may be a Custom a Mong them and be the reason why they have all in general flat, or what we call pug noses.

SATURDAY 28*th*. Mr F. and his party out Botanizing. Spent the day with the Chief and his friends much the same as yesterday.

SUNDAY 29*th*. ... After dinner we all went a Shore where a play was acted for the entertainment of such as would spend their time in looking at it. Besides the Plays which the Chief now and then caused to be acted for our entertainment there were a Set of stroling Players in the Neghbourhood who acted every day, but they were all so much of a piece that we soon grew tired of them, especially, for want of throughly knowing their Language, no intristing circumstance could be collected from them; we well know they can add to or diminish their plays at pleasure; we, our Ship and our Country they have frequently brought on the Stage, but on what account I know not. I make no doubt but it was intended as a Compliment and not interduced but when some of us were present. I generally appear'd at Oreo's Theatre towards the latter end of the Play and twice at the other in order to give my mite to the actors, the only actress was Oreo's Daughter, a pretty brown girl at whose Shrine, on these occasions, many pretty things were offered by her numerous Votarists and I believe was one great inducement why her father gave us these entertainments so often.

MONDAY 30*th*. Early in the Morning, I set out with two boats accompanied by Messrs F., Odiddy, the Chief, his Wife, Son and Daughter for an Estate which Odidde call'd his, situated at the North end of the Island, here I was promised to have Hogs and fruit in a bundance, but when we arrived I found poor Odidde could not command one single thing whatever right he might have to the Whennooa which was now in possession of his Brother, by whom were presented to me with the usual ceremony two small Hogs, in return I made him presents of three times their Value, One of the Hogs I order'd to be immidiately Kill'd and dress'd for dinner . . .

Soon after we had dined we set out for the Ship with the other Pig and a few races of Plantans which proved the sum total of our great expectations. Poor Odiddy had drank a little too freely either of the juice of peper or our Grog or both and was brought into the boat dead drunk. In our return to the Ship we put a Shore at a place where in a House we Saw four wooden Images standing upon a shelf each about 2 feet in length, they had Turbands about their heads in which were stuck some long feathers. A person in the house told us they were Eatua's no te Tou tou, that is the gods of the Common people, but this is by no means Sufficient to conclude that they worship them as such or that the Servants or Slaves are not allow'd the same Gods as those of a more elevated rank. I never heard that Tupia made any such distinction, besides these were the first wooden gods we had seen in any of the isles and all the authority we had of their being such was the bare word of, perhaps, a Superstitious person. The people of this isle are in general far more superstitious than at Otaheite or any of the other isles. The first Visit I made the chief after our arrival, he desired I would not suffer any of my people to Shoot the Heron's and Wood Pickers, Birds as Sacred to them as Robin Red-breasts, Swallows, &c^a &c^a are to many old women in England. Tupia who was a Priest, and seem'd well accquaint[ed] with their Religion, Traditions, Customs &c^a paid little or no regard to these Birds. I mention thise things because some among us were inclinable to believe that they look'd upon these two Birds as Eatua's or Gods. We fell into this opinion when I was here in the Endeavour and some others Still more Obsurd which undoubtedly we should have adopted if Tupia had not undeceived us, a Man of his knowledge we have not sence met with, concequently have added nothing to his account of their Religion but superstitious Notions.

TUESDAY 31*st*. The Natives being informed that we should sail in a few days began to bring us on board fruit more than usual, amonghest those who came on board was a young man who measured Six feet four Inches and Six-tenths, His Sister, younger than himself, measured five feet ten Inches and a half.

[...]

[June 1774]

SATURDAY 4*th*. Early in the Morn got every thing in readiness to Sail. Oreo the Chief and his whole family came to take their last leave, accompanied by Oo oorou the Aree de hi and Boba the Aree de hi of Otaha, none of them came empty handed, but Oo oorou brought a pretty large present as this was his first and only Viset, my present in return was suteable to his title, I say title because I believe he posess'd very little more. I made all the others presents sutable to their rank and the service they had done me after which they took a very affectionate leave, Oreo's last request was for me to return and when he found I would not make him the Promise, he asked the name of my *Marai* (burial place) a strange quiston to ask a Seaman, however I hesitated not one moment to tell him Stepney the Parish in which I lived when in London. I was made to repeat it several times over till they could well pronounce it, then Stepney Marai no Tootee was echoed through a hundred mouths at once. I afterwards found that the same question was put to Mr F. by a Person a Shore but he gave a different and indeed more proper Answer by saying no man who used the Sea could tell were he would be buried. It is the Custom here as well as in most other Nations for all the great families to have burial places of their own were their bones are entarr'd, these go with the estate to the next heir, as for instance at Otaheite when Toutaha held the sceptre the Marai at Oparre was Marai no Toutaha, but now they say Marai no Otoo. What greater proof could we have of these people Esteeming and loving us as friends whom they wished to remember, they had been repeatedly told we should see them no more, they then wanted to know the name of the place were our bodies were to return to dust.

As I could not promise or even Suppose that any more English Ships would be sent out to the isles our Companion Odiddee chose to remain in his Native Country, but he left us with great regret, he was a youth of good parts, of a Gentle and Humane disposision but quite ignorant of all their Traditions and Policy both in Religion and government, consequently no material knowlidge could have been got from him had I brought him away with us. Just as he was going out of the Ship he ask'd me to Tattaow some Parou[5] for him in order to Shew to any other Europeans who might touch here, I readily complied with his request by giving him a Certificate of his good behaviour, the time and were he had been with us and recommended him to the Notice of those who might come to these isles after me.

It was 11 o'Clock before we could get clear of our friends, when we weigh'd and put to Sea, but Odiddee

---

[5] Mark some speech or words – write him a testimonial, in fact.

did not leave us till we were almost out of the Harbour, in order that he might have an oppertunity to fire some of the guns, for being his Majestys Birth Day we gave them the Salute at going away. I believe I should have spent the Day with them had not my stock of Trade been wholy expended, they were continually asking for things which I had not to give them, which to me was exceeding disagreeable and made me very desireous of geting away.

When I first came to these isles I had some thoughts of Viseting the famous Island of Bola bola, but having now got all the necessary repairs of the Ship done and got a plentifull Supply of all manner of refreshments I thought it would be answering no end going there and therefore laid it a side and directed my Course to the West and took our final leave of these happy isles and the good People in them.

[. . .]

[Cook followed a course west by south towards Tonga, passing by a new island which he named Palmerston Island on 17 June.]

MONDAY 20*th. Winds East. Course S 75°30' W. Dist. Sailed 99 Miles. Lat. in South 18°50'. Longde. in West Reck.g. 168°52'. Longde. made Ulietea 17°13'.* D° gales which freshned towards Noon at which time thought we Saw Land to the ssw and accordingly hauled up for it.

TUESDAY 21*st.* *Winds East to NE. Course S 81° W. Dist. Sailed 47 Miles. Lat. in South 19°23'. Longde. in West Reck.g. 170°20'. Longde. made Ulietea 18°41'.* Gentle breezes and fair Weather. At 2 PM found what we took for land was only Clouds, reassumed our WBS Course, and an hour after saw land from the Mast head in the same direction, as we drew near found it to be an Island the body of which at 5 bore due West distant five Leagues, Shortned Sail and spent the night Plying under Top-sails. At Day break bore up for the Nother point of the Isle and ran along the West Shore at the distance of one Mile from it. A little before Noon preceiveing Some People runing along the Shore and Seeing landing was Practical, Brought-to, hoisted out and Man'd two Boats in one of which I went my self and Mr Pickersgill in the other. Mr F. and his party and Mr H. accompanied us.

WEDNESDAY 22*nd.* As we came near the Shore some People who were on the rocks retired to the woods, as we supposed to meet us and we afterwards found our conjectures right. We landed with ease and took Post on a high rock to prevent a Surprise as the whole Coast was all over run with woods, Shrubery &c^a and began to Collect plants &c^a under the protection of the Party under Arms, but the approach of the Indians soon made it necessary for us to join which was no sooner done than they appeared in the Skirts of the woods not a Stones throw from us, one of two men who were advanced before the rest threw a Stone which Struck Mr Sparman on the Arm, upon this two Musquets were fired without order which made them all retire under cover of the woods and we saw them no more. Seeing nothing was to be done here we imbarqued and proceeded down a long shore, in hopes of meeting with better Success in a nother place. We proceeded several miles down the Coast without seeing any human being or convenient landing place, at length coming before a small Beach on which lay four Canoes, here we landed by means of a small creek in the rocks, just to take a View of the Boats and to leave in them some trifles to induce the Natives to believe we intended them no harm. I left a party on the rocks under Arms to keep a good lookout while some of us went to the Canoes where we were but a few minutes before the Indians rushed out of the woods upon us, it was to no effect our endeavouring to bring them to a parly, one of them with the ferocity of a wild Boar advanced a head of the others and threw a dart at us, two or three Musquets discharged in the air did not hinder him from advanceing still farther and throwing a nother, at this instant the party on the rocks began to fire at others who appeared on the heights over us, this abated the Ardour of the party we were engaged with and gave us time to retire and then I caused the fireing to cease, the last discharge sent them into the woods from whence they did not return, we had reason to believe none were hurt. Seeing no good was to be got of these people or at the isle we return'd on board hoisted in the Boats and made sail to wsw. The Conduct and aspect of these Islanders occasioned my giving it the Name of *Savage Island*, it lies in the Latitude of 19°1',

Longitud 169°37' West, is about 11 Leagues in circuit, of a tolerable hieght and seemingly covered with wood amongest which were some Cocoa-nutt trees. These Islanders were Naked except their Natural parts, some were painted black. The Canoes were like those of Amsterdam and full as neatly made.

[...]

SATURDAY 25*th*. *Winds ENE, Calm, Northerly*. Little Clowdy and Hazey at times. In the Evening judgeing our Selves not far from Rotterdam[6] shortned Sail and spent the night under our Top-sails. At 6 AM bore away West, at Day light Saw land (Islands) extending from SSW to NNW; the Wind being at NE hauled to the NW with a view of discovering more distinctly the isles in that Quarter but presently after a reef of rocks were seen lying a thwart our Course extending on each Bow farther than we could see, it therefore became necessary to Tack and bear up to the South in search of a Passage that way. At Noon the most Southermost Isle bore SW distant about 4 Miles, near and to the North of this isle were 3 others and Several more to the west: the first four were joined to one a nother by a reef of rocks, we were not certain if this Reef did not join to the one Seen in the Morning as we saw breakers in the intermidiate space.

SUNDAY 26*th*. *Winds NE, Southerly*. At 3 PM seeing more breakers ahead and having but little wind and a

---

[6] Nomuka, among the northern Tonga (or Friendly) Islands.

great Easterly Swell, hauled off SE. In the evening the Southern isle bore WNW distant 5 miles and the Breakers last seen SSW½W; here we spent the night for it presently after fell Calm and continued so till 4 AM when we got breeze at South. At Day-light preceiving a likelyhood of a clear Passage between the Isle and the Breakers we stretched to the West and soon after saw more isles a head and on each Bow, but the Passage seem'd open; at length we found soundings in 45 & 40 fathom a clear bottom, this circumstance greatly lessned the danger sence we now had it in our power to Anchor. Towards Noon some people came off in Canoes from one of the isles bring[ing] with them some Cocoa nutts and Shaddocks which they exchanged for Nails, they shewed us Annamocka or Rotterdam . . . They like wise gave us the names of some of the other Isles and wanted us much to go to theirs. The breeze freshning we soon left them a Stern.

MONDAY 27*th*. Gentle breezes and pleasant Weather. In the PM meeting with nothing to obstruct us, at 5 o'Clock Anchored on the North side of Annamocka about ¾ of a mile from the Shore in 20 fathom water, the bottom Coral Sand, the extremes of the isle extending from S 88° E to SW and a Cove with a Sandy beach S 50° East. As soon as we approached the South end of the isle Several of the Natives came off in their Canoes one of which asked for me by name, a proof that these people have a communication with Amsterdam; as soon as we had Anchored they came a long side with yams and Shaddocks which they exchanged for Small Nails and old rags.

Early in the Morn the Master and I went a Shore to look for fresh water, we were received with great Courtesy by the Natives and conducted to a Pond of Brackish Water, the same I suppose as Tasman Water at. In the mean time those in the Boat had loaded her with fruit and roots which the Natives brought down and exchanged for Nails and Beads and on our return to the Ship found the same Traffick carrying there. After breakfast I went a Shore with two Boats to Traffick with the People and ordered the Launch to follow to take in Water. The Natives assisted us to roll the Casks to and from the Pond which was about ⅓ of a Mile, the expence of their labour was a bead or a small Nail. Fruit and roots were brought down in such plenty that the other two Boats were Laden in a trice, sent of cleared and load a second time by Noon at which time the Launch was Laden also and the Botanizing and Shooting parties all come in except the Surgeon for whom we could not wait as the Water was Ebing fast out of the Cove.

TUESDAY 28*th*. In the PM the Launch could not go for Water as there was no geting into the Cove where we landed before and where we took it off, but without the Cove is a very good landing place at all times of the Tide, here some of the Officers landed after dinner, where they found the Surgeon strip'd of his Gun, he having come to the landing place some time after the boats were gone, got a Canoe to bring him on board but he had no sooner got into her than a fellow snatched hold of the gun and ran of with it . . .

[. . .]

[*This was the start of much confusion. Cook hastened ashore to prevent precipitate retaliation, but he feared that his 'Lenity . . . incourag'd them to commit acts of greater Violence'. A watering party under Clerke was set upon and Clerke's musket and many tools were taken off. Cook went ashore again and this time seized two double canoes and fired small-shot at a protester. He got the two muskets back. The next watering party was not molested.*]

Returning from the Watering place we found some of the Natives collected together near the beach from whom we understood that the Man I had fired at was Matte (dead). I treated the Story as improbable and demanded of one of them, a man who seemed of some concequence, the return of a adze which had been taken from us in the morning and told him to send for it, accordingly two men were dispatched, but I soon found that we had quite misunderstood each other for instead of the Adze the wound'd man was brought on a board and laid down at my feet to appearance dead, but we soon found our mistake and that tho he was wounded both in the hand and thigh neither the one nor the other were dangerous. I however sent for the Surgeon a Shore to dress his wounds, in the Mean time I addressed my self to several people to have the Adze return'd, especially to an elderly woman who had always a great deal to say to me from my first landing, but upon this occasion she gave her Tongue free liberty, not one word in fifty I understood, all I could learn from her Arguments was that it was mean in me to insist on the return of so trifling an article, but when she found I was determined She and 3 or 4 more Women went away and soon after the Adze was brought me, but I saw her no more which I was sorry for as I wanted to make her a present on account of the part she seem'd to take in all our transactions, private as well as publick, for I was no sooner return'd from the Pond the first time I landed than this woman and a man presented to me a young woman and gave me to understand she was at my service. Miss, who probably had received her instructions, I found wanted by way of Handsel, a Shirt or a Nail, neither the one nor the other I had to give without giving her the Shirt on my back which I was not in a humour to do. I soon made them sencible of my Poverty and thought by that means to have come of with flying Colours but I was misstaken, for I was made to understand I might retire with her on credit, this not suteing me niether the old Lady began first to argue with me and when that fail'd she abused me, I understood very little of what she said, but her actions were expressive enough and shew'd that her words were to this effect, Sneering in my face and saying, what sort of a man are you thus to refuse the embraces of so fine a young Woman, for the girl certainly did not [want] beauty which I could however withstand, but the abuse of the old Woman I could not and therefore hastned into the Boat, they then would needs have me take the girl on board with me, but this could not be done as I had come to a Resolution not to suffer a Woman to come on board the Ship on any pretence what ever and had given strict orders to the officers to that purpose for reasons which I shall mention in a nother place.

When the Surgeon arrived he dress'd the mans wounds and let him blood and was of opinion he was in no sort of danger as the shott had done little more than penetrate the Skin. In the operation some poultice was wanting, the Surgeon ask'd for ripe Plantains but they brought Sugar Cane and Chewed it to a poulp and gave him it to apply to the wounds, this being more of a Balsamick than the other shews that these people understand Simples. After the mans wounds were dress'd I gave him a Spike Nail and a Knife which to them was of great value, his Master or at least the man who seem'd to own the Canoe took them, most probably to himself. It was rather unlucky this man did not belong to the Isle, but had lately come in one of the two Sailing Canoes from a nother isle in the Nighbourhood. Matters being once more put in order we all return'd on board to dinner.

WEDNESDAY 29*th*. Having got on board a plentifull Supply of roots and some fruits I resolved to sail as soon as we got any Wind for at present it was Calm. In the evining I went a Shore in Company with Mr F. and some of the officers, they made a little excursion into the isle but I did not quit the landing place, the Natives were every were very submissive and obligeing so that had we made a longer stay its probable we should [have] had no more reason to complain of their conduct; while I was now on Shore I got the names of Twenty Islands which lay between the NW and NE, some of them in Sight. Two which laid most to the West were remarkable on account of their great hight, in the most westermost we judged was a Vulcano by the Continual Column of Smoak we saw assend from the center of the isle; to clear up this point it was necessary we should approach them nearer, accordingly at day-light in the Morning got under Sail with a light breeze at West and Stood to the Northward for these isles, but the wind scanting carried us among the low Islots and Shoals which lie north of Annamocka so that we had to ply to windward. At Noon the middle of Annamocka bore s¼e distant 9 Miles and was at the same time close to one of the islots, those we had in Sight extended from N½W to SEBE½E, and were Sixteen or 18 in Number, the two high Islands bore from NW to NNW½W. Lat Ob^d 20°6' s. A great Number of Canoes kept about us all the forenoon; the people in them brought for Traffick Various sorts of Curiosities, some roots, fruits and fowls but of these not many; they took in exchange small Nails and Pieces of any kind of Cloth. I believe before they went away they striped the most of our people of the few Clothes the Otaheite Ladies had left them for the Passion for Curiosities was as great as ever.

THURSDAY 30*th*. The Wind being contrary and but little of it the after noon and night was spent in plying with the precaution necessary to such navigation. In the Morning Stretched out for the high Islands having the Advantage of a gentle breeze at wsw. Day no sooner dawned than we saw Canoes coming from all parts, their Traffick was much the same as yesterday or rather better, for out of one Canoe I got two Pigs which were Scarce Articles with them.

[July 1774]

FRIDAY 1st. Gentle breezes and Clowdy Weather. At 4 o'Clock in the PM we reached the two high Islands, the Southermost and the one on which the Vulcano is or is supposed to be is called by the Natives Amattafoa and the other which is round high and Peaked Oghao. We pass'd between the two, the Channell being two Miles wide, safe and without soundings; both are inhabited but neither of them appeared firtile, they lay from Annamocka NNW¼W Distant 11 or 12 Leagues. Amattafoa which is the largest of the two is about 5 Leagues in Circuit. Unfortunately the Summit of this isle during the whole day was covered with heavy clouds, so that we were not able to veryfy whether or no the Smoak we had seen was occasioned by a Vulcano or the burning of the Country, for we could see that great part of the Brow of the Hill had been consumed by fire, this divided our opinions and nothing determined. While we were in the Passage between the two Isles we had little wind, which gave time for a large Sailing Canoe which had been chasing us all day to get up with us as well as several others with Padles which had been thrown a Stern when the breeze was fresh . . .

We were hardly through the Passage before we got a fresh breeze from the South, that moment the Natives made haste to be gone and we steer'd to the west all sails set. I had some thoughts of touching at Amsterdam as it lay not much out of the way, but as the Wind was now we could not fetch it and was the occasion of my laying a side going there at all.

Before I proceed with the Sloop to the west it will be necessary to turn back to Annamocka. This Island which is situated in the Latitude of 20°15', Long^{de} 174°30' W was first discovered by Captain Tasman and by him Named Rotterdam. It is of a Triangler form each side where of is about three miles and a half or four miles, a Salt-Water Lake which is in it occupies not a sm^l part of its Surface and in a manner cuts off the SE angle. Round the isle, that is from the NW to the South, round by the North and East lies scatered a number of Islots, Sand banks and breakers, we could see no end to their extent to the North and its very probable they reach as far to the South as Amsterdam which together with Middleburg and Pylstaerts make one group of Isles, containing about three degrees in Latitude and two of Longitude: this groupe I have named the Friendly Archipelago as a lasting friendship seems to subsist among the Inhabitants and their Courtesy to Strangers intitles them to that Name. Tasman seems to have seen the northern extremity in about 19°. The Inhabitants of Boscawen and Keppels Isles, discovered by Captain Wallis in 15°53' and nearly under the same Meridian as this Archipelago, seem, from the little account I have had of them, to be the same Sort of friendly people as these. The Latitude and discriptions of these two isles point them out to be the same as Cocos and Traitors discovered by Lemaire and Schouten, but if they are the same Mr Dalrymple has placed them above 8° too far to the west in his Chart.

The Inhabitants, Productions, &c^a of Rotterdam or Annamocka and the Neighbouring isles are much the Same as at Amsterdam . . . The people of this isle seem to be more affected with the Leprous or some other Scrofulous disease than any I have yet seen, it breaks out in the face more than in any other parts of the Body. I have seen several who had quite lost their Noses by it. In one of my excursions I happen'd to peep into a house where one or more of these people were, one Man only appeared at the Door or Hole by which I was to enter and he began to Shut me out by drawing a Cord a Cross, but the intolerable Stench which came from his Putrified face was alone sufficient to keep me from entering, his Nose was quite gone and his face ruin'd being wholy covered with ulcers, or rather wholy covered with one ulcer so that the very sight of him was shocking. As our People had not quite got clear of the disease communicated to them by the women of Otaheite I took all immaginable care to prevent its being communicated to these people, and I may venture to assert that my endeavours succeeded.

[. . .]

[*Following a north-westerly course, Cook paused briefly on 3 July at Vatoa, a south-eastern islet of the Fiji group, the only contact which he made with Fiji.*]

SUNDAY 17*th*. Continued to Steer to the West till 3 o'Clock in the PM when we saw land bearing SW upon which we took in the Small Sails, reef'd the Top-sails and hauled up for it having a very Strong gale at SE thick hazey weather. At half past 5 the land bore from SSW to NWBN½W but we were not certain that we saw the whole extent either way. At half past 7 Tack'd judging our selves at this time about two leagues from the land. We stood off till between 1 and 2 in the AM then Stood in again. It was no wonder to find we had lost ground in the night for it blew exceeding hard at times and there went a great Sea from the SE, besides several of our Sails were Split and torn to pieces in the night, particularly a Fore Top-sail which was rendred quite useless as a Sail. Being desireous of geting round the Southern ends of the lands or at least so far to the South as to be able to judge of their extent in that direction, for I made no doubt but this was the Australia Del Espiritu Santo of Quiros or what M. D. Bougainville calls the Great Cyclades, and the coast we were now upon the East side of Aurora Island whose Longitude by the Observations we have lately had is 17°'E.

[. . .]

[*Cook made no landing until he reached the large island of Malekula, towards the middle of the group.*]

FRIDAY 22*nd*. Wind at SE a gentle breeze and pleasent Weather. In Standing in for the land we preceived a creek which had the appearence of a good harbour, formed by a point of land or Peninsula projecting out to the North, we just fetched this place at 1 o'Clock PM when we tack'd and stood off till half past 2 in order to gain room and time to hoist the Boats out to examine it. Several people appeared on the Point of the Peninsula and seem'd to invite us a Shore, but the most of them had Bows and Arrows in their hands. In stretching in Shore, by the help of a Tide or Current which we had not before preceived, we fetched two Leagues to windward of this place, and by that means discovered a nother opening which I sent Lieut^t Pickersgill and the Master in two Arm'd boats to Sound and look for Anchorage; Upon their makeing the Sign for the latter, we saild in and anchored in 11 fathom Water Sandy bottom, some thing more than a Cables length from the South Shore and a Mile within the entrance.

Some of the Natives came off to us in their Canoes, two of them were induced to come on board where they made a very Short stay as the Sun was already set; the kind reception these met with induced others to come off by moon light, but I would permit none to enter the Ship or even to come along-side, by this means we got rid of them for the night. They exchanged for pieces of Cloth some few Arrows, some of which were pointed with bone and diped in Poison or some green gummy substance that could Answer no other end.

In the Morning a good many came round us, some came in Canoes and others swam off. I soon prevaild on one to come on board which he had no sooner done than he was followed by more than we desired: four I took into the Cabbin and made them various presents which they Shew'd to those in the Canoes, thus a friendly intercourse between us and them was in a fair way of being opened when an accident happened which put all in confution but in the end I believe turn'd out to our advantage. A fellow in a Canoe having been refused admittance into one of our boats a long-side was going to Shoot one of the Poisoned Arrows at the Boat-keeper, some interfeering prevented him from doing it that Moment, the instant I was acquainted with this I ran on deck and saw a nother man strugling with him, one of those as I was told who were in the Cabbin and had jump'd out of the window for that purpose, but the fellow got the better of him and directed his Bow again to the boat keeper, but upon my calling to him he directed it to me and was just going to let fly when I gave him a peppering of Small Shott, this Staggered him for a Moment but did not hinder him from holding his bow in the Attitude of Shooting, another discharge of the same Nature made him drop it and the others in the Canoes to Paddle off as fast as they could. Some began to Shoot Arrows from the other side, a Musquet discharged in the air and a four pounder over their heads sent them all off in the utmost confusion; those in the Cabbin leaped out of the Windows, other that were in the ship and on different parts of the Rigging all leaped over board and many quited their Canoes and swam a shore. After this we took no further notice of them, but suffered them to come and pick up their Canoes, and some were soon after prevailed upon to come alongside. We now got every thing in readiness to land in order to try to get some refreshments, for nothing of this kind had been seen in any of their boats, and to Cut some Wood of which we were in want of.

About 9 o'Clock we landed in the face of about 4 or 500 Men who were assembled on the Shore, arm'd with Bows and Arrows, Clubs and Spears, but they made not the least opposission, on the contrary one Man gave his Arms to a nother and Met us in the water with a green branch in his hand, which [he] exchanged for the one I held in my hand, took me by the other hand and led me up to the crowd to whom I distributed Medals, Pieces of Cloth &c^a. After Mr Edgcomb had drawn his Marines up on the beach in such a manner as to Protect the workmen in cutting down wood I made Signs to the Natives that we wanted some to take on board, to which they willingly consented. A small Pigg was now brought down and presented to me for which I gave the bearer a Piece of Cloth, this gave us hopes that a trade would soon be opened for refreshments but we were misstaken, this Pig came on some other account probable as a peace offering, for all that we could say or do did not prevail upon them to bring us above half a Dozen small Cocoanutts and a small quantity of fresh water. They set no sort of Value upon Nails nor did they seem much to esteem any thing we had, they would now and then give an arrow for a Piece of Cloth but constantly refused to part with their bows, they were unwilling we should go into the Country and very desireous for us to go on board, we understood not a word they said, they are quite different to all we have yet seen and Speak a different language, they are almost black or rather a dark Chocolate Colour, Slenderly made, not tall, have Monkey faces and Woolly hair. About Noon after sending what wood we had cut on board we all embarqued and went of after which they all retired some one way and some a nother.

SATURDAY 23*rd*. Having now got on board a small quantity of Wood for present consumption and intending to put to Sea the next Morning in order to take advantage of the moonlight nights which now happened we employ'd this after-noon in seting up our lower & Top-mast Rigging which they stood in need of. Some time last night the Natives had taken away the Buoy from the Kedge Anchor we lay moor'd by, which I now saw a fellow bringing along the Strand to the landing place. I therefore took a boat and went for it accompanied by some of the Gentlemen; the moment we landed the Buoy was put into our boat by a man who walked of again without Speaking one word; it ought to be observed that this was the only thing they even so much as attempted to take from us by any means whatever and that they seem'd to Observe Strict honisty in all their dealings. Having landed near some of their houses and Plantations which were just within the Skirts of the Woods, I prevaild on one man to let me see them, they Suffered Mr F. to go with me but were unwilling any more should follow. Their houses are low and covered with thick Palm thatch, their form is oblong and some are boarded at the ends where the entrance is by a Square Port hole which at this time was Shut up; they did not chouse we should enter any of them and we attempted nothing against their inclinations; here were about half a Dozen houses, some small Plantations which were fenced round with reeds, about Twenty Piggs and a few Fowles runing about loose, and a good many fine yams lying piled up upon Sticks or kind of Platforms; here were Bread fruit Trees, Cocoa-nutt and Plantain Trees on which were little or no fruit, we afterwards saw an Orange on the beach, proof sufficient that they have of these fruit . . .

The people of this country are in general the most Ugly and ill-proportioned of any I ever saw, to what hath been allready said of them I have only to add that they have thick lips flat noses and—[7]

Their Beards as well as most of their Woolly heads are of a Colour between brown and black, the former is much brighter than the latter and is rather more of hair than wool, short and curly. The Men go naked, it can hardly be said they cover thier Natural parts, the Testicles are quite exposed, but they wrap a piece of cloth or leafe round the yard which they tye up to the belly to a cord or bandage which they wear round the waist just under the Short Ribbs and over the belly and

[7] The sentence is unfinished.

so tight that it was a wonder to us how they could endure it. They have curious bracelets which they wear on the Arm just above the Elbow, these are work'd with threed or Cord and studed with Shells and are four or five inches broad, they never would part with one, they also wear round the wrist Hoggs Tusks and rings made of large Shells; the bridge of the Nose is pierced in which they wear an ornament of this form, it is made of a stone which is not unlike alabaster, they likewise wear small ear Rings made of Tortise shell. We saw but few Women and they were full as disagreeable as the Men, their head face and Shoulders were painted with a Red Colour, they wear a piece of Cloth wraped round their Middle and some thing over their Shoulders in which they carry their Children . . .

SUNDAY 24*th*. Gentle breezes and fair Weather . . .

The Night before we came out of Port two Red fish about the Size of large Bream and not unlike them were caught with hook and line of which Most of the officers and Some of the Petty officers dined the next day. In the Evening every one who had eat of these fish were seiz'd with Violant pains in the head and Limbs, so as to be unable to stand, together with a kind of Scorching heat all over the Skin, there remained no doubt but that it was occasioned by the fish being of a Poisoness nature and communicated its bad effects to every one who had the ill luck to eat of it even to the Dogs and Hogs, one of the latter died in about Sixteen hours after and a young dog soon after shared the same fate. These must be the same sort of fish as

Quiros mentions under the name of *Pargos*, which Poisoned the Crews of his Ships, so that it was some time before they recovered. We had reason to be thankfull in not having caught more of them for if we had we should have been in the Same Situation.

[...]

[*Cook continued exploring to the south until he reached Eromanga. Here he anchored and took two boats to a sandy beach. He stepped out holding out a green branch in the face of 'a great multitude'. He 'was charmed with their behaviour', but they misinterpreted Cook's attempt to have the boats hauled up on the sand as an intention to leave, and they tried to prevent this. Fighting broke out, muskets (which kept misfiring) against darts and arrows. Back on board, Cook fired a four-pound shot as a parting gesture.*]

[*August 1774*]

FRIDAY 5*th.* . . . After leaving this Island we shaped our Course for the East end of the one to the South, being guided by a great fire we saw upon it. At 1 o'Clock we came near the Shore and made it necessary to shorten Sail and spend the remainder of the night making Short boards. At day break we discovere'd a high table land bearing EBS and a small low isle bearing NNE which we had passed in the night, Traitors head was still in sight bearing N 20° west and the Island to the Southward extending from S 7° W to S 87° W distant about one League, we now found that what we had taken for a common fire in the Night was a Volcano which threw up vast quantaties of fire and smoak and made a rumbling noise which was heard at a good distance. Soon after we had made Sail for the East end of the island we discovered an Inlet which had the appearance of a harbour, as soon as we drew near I sent two Arm'd Boats under the command of Lieut^t Cooper and the Master to examine and Sound it while we stood on and off with the Ship to be ready to follow or give them any assistance they might want. On the East point were a great number of People Hutts and Canoes, some of the latter they put into the Water and followed our boats but came not near them. It was not long before our boats made the Signal for Anchorage and we stood in accordingly: the Wind being at West, we borrowed close to the west point and pass'd over some Sunken Rocks which would been have avoided by keeping a little more to the East. The wind left us as soon as we were within the entrance and obliged us to drop an anchor in 4 fathom water when the boats were sent again to Sound and in the mean time the Launch was hoisted out and as soon as we were acquainted with the Channel, laid out warps and warped farther in. While this work was going forward Vast numbers of the Natives had collected together on the Shores and a great many came off in Canoes and some even Swam off, but came not nearer than a stones throw and those in the Canoes had their Arms in constant readiness; insensibly they became bolder and bolder and at last came under our Stern and exchanged some Cocoa nutts for pieces of Cloth &c^a; some more daring than the others were for carrying off every thing they could lay their hands upon and made several attempts to knock the rings of[f] the rudder, the greatest trouble they gave us was to look after the Buoys of our anchors which were no soon let go from the Ship or thrown out of the boats than they lay hold of them, a few Musquets fired without any design to hit had no effect, but a four pounder threw them into great confusion, made them quit their Canoes and take to the water but seeing none were hurt they presently recoverd their fright and returned to their Canoes and once more attempted to take away the buoys, this put us to the necessity of firing a few Musketoon shot over them which had the desired effect and altho none were hurt they were afterwards afraid to come near them and at last retired to the Shore and we were suffered to set down to dinner undisturbed. During these transactions a friendly old man in a small Canoe made several trips between us and the shore, bringing with him 2 or 3 Cocoa nutts or a yam each time and took in exchange what ever we gave him: another was on the gang way when the great gun was fired, but he was not to be prevailed upon to stay long after.

SATURDAY 6*th*. Wind at South a fresh breeze and fair weather. In the PM after the Ship was moor'd I landed with a strong party of Men at the head of the harbour without any opposition being made by a great number of the islanders assembled in two parties the one on our right and the other on our left, all arm'd with darts, clubs, slings, bows and arrows: after our men were drawn up upon the beach I distributed to the old people presents of pieces of Cloth, Medals &c^a and ordered two Casks of Water to be fill'd out of a Pond which we found conveniently situated behind the beach, giving the Natives to understand it was what we wanted. We got from them a few Cocoa-nuts which seem'd to be in plenty on the trees, but they would not on any account part with any of their Arms which they held in constant readiness and press'd so much upon us that little was wanting to make them attack us, however no attempt was made, our early embarqueing probably disconcerted their scheme and after that they all retired.

I now found it was practical to lay the Ship nearer to the landing place, and as we wanted to take in a large quantity of both wood and Water it would greatly facilitate that work as well as over-awe the Natives and be more ready to assist our people on Shore in case of an attack, we therefore in the morning went to work to transport her: while this was doing we observed the Natives assembling from all parts to the landing or Watering place where they form'd themselves into two parties one on each side the landing place, we judged there were not less than a thousand people arm'd in the same manner as in the evening. A Canoe conducted some times by one and at other times by 2 or 3 Men would now and then come off from them, invite us to go a Shore and bring us a few Cocoa-nuts or Plantains which they gave without asking for any thing in return but I took care they always had some thing. One of those who came off was the old man whose behaviour had attracted our attention yesterday. I gave him to understand by Signs (for we could not understand one another) that they were to lay a side their Arms, took those which were in his Canoe and threw them over board, there was no doubt but he understood me and I believe made it known to his country men on shore for as soon as he landed he went first to the one party and then to the other, and as to himself he was never after seen with any thing like a weapon in his hand. Three fellows coming under the Stern in a Canoe offered a Club for a String of beads and some other trifles all of which I sent down to them, but the Moment they were in their possession they padled off in all haste without makeing any return, this was what I expected and what I was not sorry for as I wanted a pretence to shew the Multitude on shore the effect of our fire arms without materially hurting any of them, having a Musquet ready load[ed] with Small Shott, (N° 3) I gave one of the fellows the Contents into the bargin and when they were above Musquet shott off, order'd 3 or 4 Musketoons or Wall pieces to be fired at them which made them quit the Canoe and keep under her off side and swim with her to the shore, this trans-action seem'd to have little or no effect on the two divisions on shore, on the contrary they seem'd to think it sport.

After mooring the Ship by four anchors with her broad side to the landing place, from which she was hardly Musquet Shott, and placeing our Artillery in such a manner as to command the whole harbour, we embarked the Marines and a party of Seamen in three boats and rowed in for the Shore; I have already observed that the two divisions of the Natives were drawn up on each side the landing place, the space between was 30 or 40 yards, here were laid to the most advantage a few bunches of plantains, a yam and two Tara roots, between them and the shore were stuck in the sand four small reeds about 2 feet from each other in a line at right angles to the sea shore, for what purpose they were put there I never could learn; the old man before mentioned and two more stood by these things and by Signs invited us a Shore, but we were not in a hurry to land, I had not forgot the trap I had like to have been caught in at the last isle and this looked some thing like it; we answered the old men by makeing signs that the two divisions must retire farther back and give us more room, the old men seem'd to desire them so to do but as little regard was paid to them as us. More were continually joining them, and except the 3 old men, not one was without arms: In short every thing conspired to make us believe they intended to attack us as soon as we were on shore. The consequence of such a step was easily seen, many of them must have been kill'd and wounded and we should hardly have escaped unhurt. Sence therefore they would not give us the room we required I thought it was best to frighten them away rather than oblige them by the deadly effect of our fire Arms and accordingly order a Musquet to be fired over the heads of the party on our right for this was by far the Strongest body, the alarm it gave them was only momentary, in an instant they recovered themselves and began to display their weapons, one fellow shewed us his back side in such a manner that it was not necessary to have an interpreter to explain his meaning; after this I ordered three or four more to be fired, this was the Signal for the Ship to fire a few four pound Shott over them which presently dispersed them and then we landed and marked out the limits on the right and [left] by a line. Our old friend stood his ground all the time, tho' diserted by his two companions, the moment we landed I made him a present of Cloth and other things I had taken with me for the purpose. Insencibly the Natives came to us seemingly in a more friendly manner, some even came without arms, but by far the greatest part brought them and when we made signs to them to lay them down, they told us to lay down ours first; they climed the Cocoa trees and threw us down the Nutts, without requiring any thing for their trouble, but we took care they were always paid. After filling half a doz^n Small Casks with Water and obtaining leave of the old man whose name was [Paowang] to cut wood for fireing, just to let the people see what we wanted we return'd on board to dinner after which they to a man retired. I never learnt that any one of them was hurt by our Shott.

SUNDAY 7*th*. . . . In the night the Volcano threw up vast quantities of fire and Smoak, the flames were seen to ascend above the hill between us and it, the night before it did the same and made a noise like that [of] thunder or the blowing up of mines at every eruption which happened every four or five Minutes; a heavy shower of rain which fell at this time seem'd to increase it: the wind blew from that quarter and brought such vast quantities of fine Sand or ashes that every thing was covered with it, and was also exceeding troublesom to the eyes . . .

[. . .]

WEDNESDAY 10*th*. . . . Yesterday Mr Forster obtained from these people the Name of the Island (Tanna) and to day I got from them the names of those in the nieghbourhood. They gave us to understand in such a manner which admited of no doubt that they eat human flesh, they began the subject themselves by asking us if we did: they like wise gave us to understand that Circumcision was practised amongest them. While the Launch was taking in ballast on the West side of the harbour, one man employed on this work scalded his fingers in takeing up a stone out of some water, this circumstance produced the discovery of several hot springs at the foot of the clift rather below high-water mark. In the AM Mr F. and his party made an excursion into the country, he met with civil treatment from the Natives and saw several fine Plantations of Plantains, Sugar Cane, roots &c^a. The people now, especially those in our neighbourhood are so well reconciled to us that they take no notice of our going a Shooting in the woods.

THURSDAY 11*th*. Wind at South with some heavy showers of rain in the night. In the PM two or three boy's got behind some thickets and threw 2 or 3 stones at our people, who were cuting wood, for which they were fired at by the petty officers present. I was much displeased at such an abuse of our fire Arms and took measures to prevent it for the future. During the night and all the next day the Volcano made a terrible noise throwing up prodigeous colums of Smoak and fire at every erruption; at one time great stones were seen high in the air. In the AM beside the necessary work of Wooding and Watering, we struck the main-top-mast in order to fix new Tristle-trees and a pair of new back stays. Mr F. made a little excursion up the hill on the west side the harbour where he found three places from whence assended Smoak or Steam of a Sulpherous smell, they seem'd to keep pace with the Volcano, for at every erruption the quantity of smoak or steam was greatly increased and forced out of the ground in such quantities as to be seen at a great distance which we had before taken for the smoak of common fire; it is at the foot of this hill the hot springs before mentioned are.

FRIDAY 12*th*. In the After-noon Mr F. carried his botanical excursions to the other side of the harbour and fell in with Paowang's house where he saw most of the articles I had given him hanging on the adjoining bushes, probably they were in his eyes of so little Value as not to be worth house room. Some of the gentlemen accompanied Mr F. to the hot places he was at yesterday. [A thermometer] placed in a little hole made in one of them rose from 80 to 170. Several other parts of the hill emitted Smoak or Steam all the day, the Volcano was unusally furious and filled all the circumjacent air with its ashes so that the drops of rain which fell was mixed with its ashes, it mattered not which way the wind blew we were sure to be troubled with them. The Natives gave us now very little trouble and we made little excursions inland with safety, they would however have been better pleased if we had confined our selves to the Shore, as a proof of this, some of them undertook to conduct the gentlemen to a place where they might see the mouth of the Volcano, they very readily embraced the offer and were conducted down to the harbour before they preceived the cheat.

[...]

SUNDAY 14*th*. Wind northerly, weather as yesterday. After breakfast we made up a party consisting of 9 or 10 and set out in order to see if we could not have a nearer and better View of the Volcano, we first went to one of those burning or hot places before mentioned having a Thermometer with us we made a hole in the ground where the greatest heat seem'd to be into which we put it; in the open air the mercury stood at [?] but here it presently rose to and stood at [210] which is only two below boiling Water. The Earth in this place was a kind of Pipe clay or whitish marl which had a sulpherous smell and was soft and wet, the upper surface only excepted which was crusted over with a thin dry crust, on which was Sulpher and a Vitriolick substance which tasted like Alumn: the whole space was no more than eight or ten yards square, near to which were some fig-trees who spread their branches over a part of it ... Happening to turn out of the common path we came into a plantation where there was a Man at work, he either out of good Nature or to get us the sooner out of his territories, undertook to be our guide, we had not gone with him far before we met a nother fellow standing at the junction of two roads with a Sling and a Stone in his hand, both of which he thought proper to lay aside when a Musquet was pointed at him, the Attitude we found him in and the ferosity which appear'd in his looks and his beheavour after, led us to think he meant to defend the path he stood in; he pointed to the other along which he and our guide led us, he counted us several times over and kept calling for assistance and was presently joined by two or three more one of which was a young Woman with a Club in her hand; they presently conducted us to the brow of a hill and pointed to a road which led down to the harbour and wanted us to go that way, we refused to comply and returned to the one we had left which we pursued alone our guide refusing to go with us; after assending a nother ridge as closely covered with Wood as those we had come over, we saw still other hills between us and the Volcano which discouraged us from proceeding farther especially as we could get no one to be our guide and therefore came to a resolution to return, we had but just put this into execution when we met twenty or thirty of the Natives collicted together and were close at our heels, we judged their design was to oppose our advancing into the Country but now they saw us returning they suffered us to pass unmolested and some of them put us into the right road and accompanied us down the hill, made us to stop in one place where they brought us Cocoa nutts, Plantains and Sugar Canes and [what] we did not eat on the spot, brought down the hill for us; thus we found these people Civil and good Natured when not prompted by jealousy to a contrary conduct, a conduct one cannot blame them for when one considers the light in which they must look upon us in, its impossible for them to know our real design, we enter their Ports without their daring to make opposition, we attempt to land in a peaceable manner, if this succeeds its well, if not we land nevertheless and mentain the footing we thus got by the Superiority of our fire arms, in what other light can they than at first look upon us but as invaders of their Country; time and some acquaintance with us can only convince them of their mistake.

MONDAY 15*th*. In the PM I made an excursion in company with Mr Wales on the other side of the harbour, where we met from the Natives very different treatment [from what] we had done in the morning, these people, in whose neighbourhood lived our friend Paowang, being better acquainted with us than those we had seen in the morning, shewed a readiness to oblige us in every thing in their power: here was a little Stragling Village consisting of a few houses which need no other discription than to compare them to the roof of a thatched house taken of the walls and placed on the ground, the figure was oblong and open at both ends, some indeed had a little fence or wall of reeds at each end about 3 feet high, some seem'd to be intended for more families than one as they had a fire place near each end, there [were] other mean and small hovels which I understood were only to Sleep in, in one of these which with some others stood in a Plantation but separated from them by a fence, I understood was a dead Corps, they made Signs that he slipt or was dead, circumstances sufficiently pointed out the latter. Curious however to see all I could I prevailed on an elderly man to go with me within the fence which surrounded it, one end of the hut was closed up the same as the sides the other end had been open but now shut up with Matts which he would not suffer me to remove, he also seem'd unwilling I should look into a Matted bag or basket which hung to the end of the hutt, in which was a piece of roasted yam and some kind of leaves all quite fresh: thus I was led to believe that these people dispose of the dead some thing in the same manner as at Otaheite. The Man had about his neck fastned to a String two or three locks of human hair and a Woman present had several; I offered some thing in exchange for them but they gave me to understand this could not be done as they belonged to the person who laid in the hutt. A similar custom to this is observed by the New Zealanders. Near most of their larger houses are placed upright in the ground in a square position about 3 feet from each other the Stems of four Cocoa-nut trees, some of our gentlemen who first saw these seem'd to think they had a Religious tendancy, but I was now fully satisfied they were to hang cocoa upon to dry. Thier houses are generally built in an open Area where the air has a free circulation, in some are a large tree or two whose spreading branches afford an agreeable shade and retreat from the Scorching Sun . . .

TUESDAY 16*th*. Winds northerly fair Weather. In the PM Mr F. and I took a Walk to the Eastern Sea shore in order to have a sight of an Island to the SE which these People called Annattom; the high table Island we discovered the Morning we anchored here is called Irromang or Foottoona and the flat isle lying off the harbour Immer. I observed that in their Sugar Plantations were dug holes or Pitts about 4 feet deep and 5 or six in diameter, we were made to understand that these Pitts were to catch Ratts which when once in they could not get out and so were easy killed, these animals which are distructive to the Canes are here in plenty. In the Morning after having got every thing in readiness to put to Sea and waited for nothing but a wind we found the Tiler sprung and other ways deffective in the Rudder head and by some strange neglect we had never a spare one on board and this was not known till now we wanted it. While the Carpenter was unshiping the old tiler I went ashore to cut down a tree to make a new one, but as we knew but of one fit for the purpose which stood near the watering place and this Paowang had disired might not be cut down and I had promised it should not proper application was therefore necessary in order not to give umbrage to the Natives. Therefore as soon as I landed I sent for old Paowang and as soon as he came made him a present of a Dog and a large piece of Cloth and then made known to him that our great steering Paddle was broke and that I wanted that tree to make a new one, he presently gave his consent as well as several others present and we set people to work to cut it down. It was easy to see that this Method which I took to Obtain the tree was very agreeable to all the people present. After this I returned on board with Paowang who stayed dinner. After the tiler was unshiped we found that by scarfing a piece to the inner end and liting it farther into the rudder head it would still perform its office and the Carpenters and smiths were set about this work . . .

[. . .]

THURSDAY 18*th*. In the PM Mr F. and I went to the west side of the Harbour to try the degree of heat of the hot Springs, in one of which the mercury in the Thermometer rose to 191 from 78 which it stood at in the open air. At this time it was high-water and within two or three feet of the spring which we judged might be in some degree cooled by it but the next morning we found just the contrary for repeting the experiment when the tide was out the Mercury rose no higher than 187, but at a nother Spring which bubbles out in large quantities from under a steep rock at the SW corner of the harbour, the Mercury rose to 202½ which is only 9½ below boiling water; I have already said that these Springs are at the foot of the same hill on the side of which we saw the hot places and Smokes ascend before mentioned: this hill belongs to the Same Ridge in which the Volcano is: the Ridge is of no great height nor is the Volcano at the highest part of it but on the SE side and contrary to the Opinion of Philosophers, which is that all Volcanos must be at the summits of the highest hills, here are hills in this island more than double the height of the ridge I have been speaking of. Nor was the Volcano on the isle of Ambrrym (which I now have not the least doubt of there being one if not two) on the highest part of the Island but seem'd to us to be in a Vally between the hills: to these remarks must be added [a] nother which is that during wet or moist weather the Volcano was most vehement. Here seems to be [a] feild open for some Philosophical reasoning on these extraordinary Phenomenon's of nature, but as I have no tallant that way I must content my self with stateing facts as I found and leave the causes to men of more abilities.

FRIDAY 19*th*. Winds northerly a gentle gale. In [the PM] the Tiller was finished and Shiped, so that we only waited for a fair Wind to put to sea. In the AM as the wind would not admit of our geting to sea I sent the guard on [shore] with Mr Wales as usual and at the same time a party to cut up and bring off the remainder of the tree we had cut a spare tiller of. A good many of the Natives were, as usual, assembled near the landing place and unfortunately one of them was Shott by one of our Centinals;[8] I who was present

[8] The marine, William Wedgeborough. He had earlier been punished for drunkenness and for 'easing himself betwixt decks'. He fell overboard and was drowned off Tierra del Fuego.

and on the Spot saw not the least cause for the commiting of such an outrage and was astonished beyond
Measure at the inhumanity of the act, the rascal who
perpetrated this crime pretended that one of the
Natives laid his arrow across his bow and held it in the
Attitude of Shooting so that he apprehen[d]ed himself
in danger, but this was no more than what was done
hourly and I believe with no other View than to let us
see they were Armed as well as us: what made this
affair the more unfortunate it not appearing to be the
man who bent the Bow but a nother who was near
him.[9] After this unhappy affair most of the Natives
fled and when we imbarked to go on board they retired
to a man and only a few appeared in the afternoon . . .
During the night the Wind Veered round to SE. At
4 AM began to unmoor and at 8 got under sail and
Stood out to Sea, leaving the Launch behind to take
up a Kedge Anchor and hawser we had out to cast by
and was obliged to Slip. As soon as were clear of the
harbour we brought-to to wait for the Launch and to
hoist her and the other boats in which was employment
till Noon, when we made Sail and Stretched to the
Eastward with our Starboard tacks on board in order
to take a nearer View of the Island of Erronan the
same as we discover'd in the morning of the 5th.

[. . .]

[9] Cook had Wedgeborough brought to the gangway to be flogged,
but he was dissuaded by the officers on the grounds that the marine
had been acting on the orders of his lieutenant, John Edgecumbe.

[*Cook went south round Tanna then north, spending the rest of August exploring the New Hebrides archipelago, circumnavigating the northern island which Quirós had named Austrialia del Espiritu Santo in 1606. On 1 September he began the voyage south towards New Zealand. On 5 September James Colnett saw land, a new land which Cook later took possesion of under the name of New Caledonia. The people 'spoke a language quite new to us', but were very cooperative in the matter of fresh water. 'No people could behave with more civility than they did.' Cook thought that the island, with its mountains, streams, plantations, 'little Stragling Villages', woods and beaches, 'might afford a Picture for romance'. Exploration of the coastline on the eastern side was particularly difficult because of reefs and shoals. At the south-eastern extremity tall objects on a number of islands caused great puzzlement. On closer inspection 'every one were now satisfied they were trees, except our Philosophers [the Forsters], who still maintained they were Stone Pillars'. They had discovered the great* Araucaria columnaris *– or Cook pine, which Cook and his carpenter thought ideal for ships' masts. On 10 October, as they made their way towards New Zealand, they discovered an uninhabited island which Cook named Norfolk Isle. Cook noted again a source for masts in its magnificent trees. Then for Queen Charlotte Sound, 'there to refresh my people and to put the Ship in a condition to cross this great ocean in a high Latitude once more'.*]

[October 1774]

MONDAY 17*th*. PM Fresh gales Northerly and Cloudy weather. At 4 Sound^d no ground with a line of 140 fathoms. Middnight heavy Squalls with rain, Thunder and Lightning. Wind shifted to SW, remain'd unsetled: Split the Jibb to pieces, lost great part of it, remains good for little, being much worn. Day-break saw Mount Egmont (covered with everlasting snow) bearing SE½E; sounded 70 fathoms, muddy bottom, distance off shore 3 Leagues. Wind Westerly a fresh gale, Steer'd SSE for Queen Charlottes Sound. Noon Cape Egmont ENE distant 3½ or 4 leagues, the Mount hid in the Clouds, judged it to be in one with the Cape. Lat Ob^d 39°24' Long^{de} in [Watch 173°1'].

TUESDAY 18*th*. Very strong gales at Westerly and Cloudy. Steered SEE for Queen Charlottes Sound. At 7 Close reefed the Fore & Main Top-sails and handed the Mizen Top-sail, got down Top g^t yards and hauled the wind close. At 11 Stephens's Isle SEBE. At middnight Tacked and made a trip to the North till 3 AM then bore up for the Sound under double reef'd Topsails and Courses. At 9 hauled round point Jackson through a Sea which looked Terrible, occasioned by the Tide, Wind & Sea, but as we knew the Cause it did not alarm us; At 11 Anchored before Ship Cove the strong fluries from the land not permiting us to get in.

WEDNESDAY 19*th*. PM As we could not move the Ship I went into the Cove to try to catch some fish with the Sein. As soon as I landed I looked for the bottle I had left behind in which was the Memd^m it was gone, but by whom it did not appear. Two hauls with the Sein procured us only four small fish, after shooting a few old Shags and robing the Nests of some young ones we returned aboard. AM being little wind, weighed and Warped into the Cove and there moored a Cable each way, Intending to wait here to refresh the Crew, refit the Ship in the best manner we could and compleat her with Wood and Water. We unbent the Sails to repair several having been much damage'd in the late gale, the Main and Fore Course, already worn to the utmost, was condemned as useless. Struck and unriged the Fore and Main Topmasts to fix moveable Cheeks to them for want of which the Trestle trees were Continually breaking. Set up the Forge to make bolts for the above use and repair what was wanting in the Iron way. Set up the Astronomers Observatory on shore in the bottom of the Cove and Tents for the reception of a Guard, Sail-makers, Coopers &c^a. Ordered Vegetable, of which here were plenty, to be boiled with Oatmeal & Portable Soup every Morning for breakfast and with Pease and Portable Soup every day to dinner for all hands. We now found that some Ship had been here sence we last left it not only by the bottle being gone as mentioned above, but by several trees having been Cut down with Saws and Axes which were standing when we sailed. This Ship could be no other than the Adventure Captain Furneaux.

THURSDAY 20*th*. PM Fresh gales at NW and fair weather. Sent all the Sails wanting repairs a Shore to the Tent and in the AM several empty Casks. Carpenters employed fixing Cheeks to the Top-masts, Caulkers caulking the sides and Seamen overhauling the rigging. Winds Southerly Hazey Cloudy weather.

FRIDAY 21*st*. Wind Southerly with continual rain.

SATURDAY 22*nd*. First part D° Weather, remainder Clear pleasant weather, which admited us to go on with our works and for my self and the Botanists to viset several parts of the Sound and a mongest others our gardens on Motouara which we found allmost in a state of Nature and had been wholy neglected by the Inhabitants, nevertheless many Articles were in a florishing state. None of the Natives having as yet made their appearence we made a fire on the isle, judgeing the smoke would draw their attention towards us.

SUNDAY 23*rd*. Variable light airs and pleasant weather. Every one who chused were at liberty to go a shore.

MONDAY 24*th*. Pleasant weather. AM went on with the various works in hand. Two Canoes were seen coming down the Sound but retired behind a point on the west side upon discovering us as was supposed. After breakfast I went in a Boat to look for them accompani'd by the Botanists. As we proceeded a long shore we shott sever[l] birds, the report of our guns gave notice of our approach and the Natives discovered them selves by hollaing to us but when we came before their habitations only two men appeared on a rising ground, the rest had taken to the Woods and hills, but the moment we landed they knew us again, joy took place of fear, they hurried out of the woods, embraced us over and over and skiped about like Mad men. I made them presents of Hatchets, Knives, Cloth & Medals and in return they gave us a quantity of fish. There were only one or two amongest them whose faces we could well recolect, the account they gave us of our other friends whom we inquir'd after by name were variously understood concequently ended in nothing. After a short Stay we took leave and returned aboard, they promiseing to come to the Ship in the Morning and bring with them fish which was all I wished for by the intercourse.

TUESDAY 25*th*. Winds sw pleasent Weather. Early in the Morning our friends paid us a Viset and brought with them a quantity of fish which they exchanged for Otaheite cloth &c^a and then returned to their habitations.

WEDNESDAY 26*th*. PM fresh gales Southerly with rain. AM Variable light Airs and fair Weather. The Carpenters had no sooner finished the Cheeks to the Topmasts than we found one of the fore Cross-trees broke, set them to work to make a new one out of the Spare Anchor Stock. Got into the after hold four Launch Load of Shingle ballast and struck down Six guns from off the Deck, keeping no more than Six Mounted. Our good friends the Natives stick by us and supply us plentifully with fish.

THURSDAY 27*th*. Variable gentle breezes and pleasent weather, favourable for the carrying on of our works which increase upon us the more we examine and look into things.

FRIDAY 28*th*. PM Wind and Weather as before. AM fresh gale Westerly fair weather. Rigged and fidded the Topg^t Masts. Went on a Shooting party to the west bay, Viseted the place where I left the Hogs and fowls, saw no vestige's of them or of any people being there sence. Viseted some of the Natives who gave us some fish in return for some trifles I gave them. Soon after we left them Mr F. thought he heard the squeaking of a Pig in the woods hard by their habitations, probably they may yet have those they had when we were last here. Returned on board with about a Doz^n and a half of Wild fowl, Shaggs and Sea Pies. Sence the Natives have been with us a report has risen said to come first from them, that a ship has lately been lost, some where in the Strait, and all the crew Killed by them, when I examined them on this head they not only denied it but seem'd wholy ignorant of the matter.

[. . .]

SUNDAY 30*th*. Wind Southerly a fresh gale with showers of rain. Natives a board most of the day tradeing with green talk, hatchets &c^a. One of the officers found in the Woods not far from our tents a fresh hens egg, a proof that the Poultry that we left here are living, the Natives tell us that they lost those I gave them in the Woods.

MONDAY 31*st*. AM Wind at NE fine pleasent weather. Our Botanists went to Long Island where some of the party saw a Hog, a boar as they judged, so wild that it took to the woods as soon as it saw them. It is probably one of those Captain Furneaux left behind and brought to this isle by the Natives. Sence the Natives did not distroy these Hogs when in their posession, we cannot suppose they will attempt it now, so that there is little fear but that this Country will soon be stocked with these Animals, both in a wild and domistick state. I am in doubt that the goats I put ashore are killed, for if they killed the goats why should they not the hogs also.

[...]

[November 1774]

THURSDAY 3*rd*. Variable light breezes and pleasent weather. Fided the Main Top-mast and set up the Main & Top-mast rigging. Compleated the Ship with Wood and Water and nearly finished all our other works except Caulking which goes on slowly, as having only two Caulkers and a great deal to do and which must absolutely be done before we can put to sea.

FRIDAY 4*th*. Fine pleasent Weather. Most of the Natives retired up the Sound to their habitations there. Went over to Long Island to look for the Hog which had been seen there, found it to be one of the Sows Captain Furneaux left behind the same as was in the posession of the Natives when we were last here. From a Supposion of its being a boar I had carri'd over a Sow to leave with him but brought her back when I found the Contrary.

SATURDAY 5*th*. Light breeze Westerly and pleasent Weather. Early in the morning our old friend[s] paid us a second Viset and brought us a supply of fish. At 8 o'Clock went in the Pinnace up the Sound accompanied by Mr F. and his party. I had some thoughts of finding the termination of it or to see if it communicated with the sea, in our way we met with several people out fishing of whom we made the necessary enquiries, they all agree'd that there was no passage to Sea by the head of the Sound. After proceeding five Leagues up, which was farther than I had ever been before, we met a Canoe conducted by four or five men who confirm'd what the others had told us; we then enquired if their was any passage to the East and understood them there was, this was what I suspected for from the Hill I first discovered the Strait I saw a Bason into which the tide had access & recess, but I did not know whether it was an Arm of the Sound or an inlet of the Sea; to determine this point I laid aside the scheme of proceeding to the head of the Sound and went to this Inlet, which is on the SE side of the Sound four or five leagues above Ship Cove, here we found a large settlement of the Natives who received us with great courtesy; our stay with them was short as we found incouragement to persue the object we had in view and accordingly proceeded ENE down the Inlet which we at last found to open into the Sea by a Channell about a mile wide in which ran a very strong tide. It was four o'Clock in the after noon before we had made this discovery which opens a new passage into the Sound and as we came to a resolution to return aboard that same evening we were obliged to defer viseting a large Hippa or strong hold built on a rising ground on the North side a little within the entrance whose inhabitants seem'd to invite us to them and without makeing any stop proceeded for the Ship which [we reached] by 10 o'Clock bring[ing] with us some fish we had got from the Natives and a few birds we had shott, amongest which were some of the same sort of Ducks we got in Duskey Bay and we have reason to think they are all to be found here as the Inhabitants of this place have a particular [name] to each.

SUNDAY 6*th*. Wind NE, Gloomy weather with some rain. Had a present from one of the Natives whose name was *Pedero* of a Staff of honour, in return I dress'd him in an old suit of Clothes with which he was not a little proud: having got him and a nother in a communicative mood we began to enquire of them if the Adventure had been here and they gave us to understand in a manner which admited of no doubt that soon after we were gone she arrived and Stayed here about [?] Days, and farther asserted that neither her or any other Ship had been Stranded on the Coast as had been reported. After breakfast I took a number of men over to Long Island to endeavour to catch the Sow but we returned without being able to see her. [Pedero] dined with us, eat of every thing at table and drank more Wine than any of us.

MONDAY 7*th*. A fresh gale at NE attended with rain which put a stop to Calking.

TUESDAY 8*th*. First part rain remainder fair weather which enabled us to go on with Calking, the Seams we are obliged to pay with a kind of putty made of Cooks fat and Chalk, for as to Pitch and Tarr we have had none for some Monthes Past and a Cask of Varnish of Pine which served as a substitute for all purposes is now expended. Put two Piggs, a Boar and a sow a Shore in the Cove next without Cannibal Cove, its hardly possible for all the methods I have taken to stock this Country with these animals to fail.

WEDNESDAY 9*th*. Winds Westerly or NW, Squally with rain, got every thing off from the Shore, unmoor'd and hove short on the best bower, waiting for the Calkers to finish their work. Our friends the Natives brought us a seasonable and large supply of fish. I made my friend [Pedero] a present of an Oyle Jarr which made him as happy as a prince.

THURSDAY 10*th*. Fresh gales at NW and fair weather. PM hove up the anchor and drop'd out of the Cove and then anchored in a clear place for the more readier geting under-sail in the morning. After this a party of us spent the afternoon a shore, we land where were two families of the Natives, variously employed, some sleeping, others makeing Matts, dressing Victuals &c^a. One little girl I observed was heating stones at a fire, curious to know what they were for I remained by her, for I thought they were to dress some sort of Victuals but I was misstaken for as soon as the stones were made hot, the girl took them hout of the fire and gave them to an hold Women who was siting in the hut, she put them in [a] heap and then laid over them a large handfull of green Sellery, over it a coarse Mat and then squated herself down upon her heels over all, thus she made what one may call a Dutch Warming-Pan on which she sit as close as a hare to her seat.

At Daylight AM weighed and stood out of the Sound with a gentle breeze at WNW. At 8 hauled round the two brothers and steered for Cape Campbel which is at the SE entrance of the Strait.

FRIDAY 11*th*. In the morning the wind veered round by the west to South and forced us more to the East than I intended. At 7 o'Clock in the evening the Snowey Mountains bore WBS and Cape Palliser North ½ west dist^t 16 or 17 leagues. From this Cape I shall, for the third time, take my departure. After a few hours calm a breeze sprung up at North with which we steered SBE all sails Set, with a view of geting into the

Latitude of 54° or 55°. My intention was to cross this vast Ocean nearly in these Parallels, and so as to pass over those parts which were left unexplored last summer.

[...]

[*For two weeks the* Resolution *sailed south east and then east without incident.*]

SATURDAY 26*th* and SUNDAY 27*th*. Had a steady fresh gale at NNW with which Steered East and at Noon on the latter we were in the Latitude of 55°6', Longitude 138°56' west. I now gave up all hopes of finding any more land in this Ocean and came to a Resolution to steer directly for the West entrance of the Straits of Magelhanes, with a View of coasting the out, or South side of Terra del Fuego round Cape Horn to Strait La Maire. As the world has but a very imperfect knowledge of this Coast, I thought the Coasting it would be of more advantage to both Navigation and Geography than any thing I could expect to find in a higher latitude. In the after-noon of this day the Wind blew in squalls and occasioned the Main Topg^t mast to be carried away.

MONDAY 28*th*. A very strong gale Northerly, hazy rainy weather which obliged us to double reef the Fore and Main Top-sails, hand the Mizen Top-sail and get down the Fore Top-g^t yard. In the morn^g the bolt rope of the Main Top-sail broke and occasioned the Sail to be split. I have observed that the ropes to all our sails, the Square Sails especially, are not of a Size and strength sufficient to wear out the canvas. At Noon Latitude in 55°20', Longitude 134°16' west. A great swell from NW. Albatrosses and Blue Peterels seen.

[...]

[December 1774]

FRIDAY 16*th*. In the Latitude of 53°25', Longitude 78°40' it was 17°38' East. About this time saw a Penguin and a piece of weed and the next morn a Seal and some diving Peterels. For the three preceeding days the wind has been at west a steady fresh gale, attended now and then with showers of rain or hail.

SATURDAY 17*th*. At 6 o'Clock in the Morning, being nearly in the same latitude as above and in the Longitude of 77°10' W the Variation was 18°33' E, and in the after-noon it was 21°38', Latitude in at that time 53°16' S, Longitude 75°9' West. In the Morning as well as in the after-noon I took some observations to determine the Longitude by the Watch, the results reduced to noon gave 76°18'30" West Longitude: at the same time the Longitude by my reckoning was 76°17' W, but I have reason to think that we were about half a degree more to the West than either the one or the other: our Latitude at the same time was 53°21' S. We steered EBN and E½N all this day under all the sail we could carry with a fine fresh gale at NWBW in expectation of seeing the land before night but not making it before 10 o'Clock we took in the Studding sails, Topg^t Sails, and a reef in each Top-sail and steered ENE in order to make sure of falling in with Cape Deseado. Two hours after made the land, extending from NEBN to EBS about 6 Leagues dist^t. Upon this discovery we wore and brought to with the ships head to the South and then sounded and found 75 fathoms water, the bottom stones and shells. The land now before us can be no other than the west Coast of Terra del Fuego and near the West entrance to the Straits of Magelhanes. As this was the first run that had been made directly a Cross this ocean in a high Sothern Latitude.[10] I have been a little particular in noteing every circumstance that appeared attall Intresting and after all I must observe that I never was makeing a passage any where of such length, or even much shorter, where so few intresting circumstance[s] occured, for if I except the Variation of the Compass I know of nothing else worth notice. The weather has neither been unusually Stormy nor cold, before we arrived in the Latitude of 50° the Mercury in the Thermometer fell gradually from 60 to 50 and after we arrived in the Latitude of 55° it was generally between 47 and 45, once or twice it fell to 43°; these observations were made at Noon. I have now done with the SOUTHERN PACIFIC OCEAN, and flatter my self that no one will think that I have left it unexplor'd, or that more could have been done in one voyage towards obtaining that end than has been done in this.

[10] Cook here inserted a conscientious footnote: 'It is not to be supposed that I could know at that time that the Adventure had made the Passage before me.'

THE STORY OF PENGUIN CLASSICS

Before 1946 …'Classics' are mainly the domain of academics and students, without readable editions for everyone else. This all changes when a little-known classicist, E. V. Rieu, presents Penguin founder Allen Lane with the translation of Homer's *Odyssey* that he has been working on and reading to his wife Nelly in his spare time.

1946 *The Odyssey* becomes the first Penguin Classic published, and promptly sells three million copies. Suddenly, classic books are no longer for the privileged few.

1950s Rieu, now series editor, turns to professional writers for the best modern, readable translations, including Dorothy L. Sayers's *Inferno* and Robert Graves's *The Twelve Caesars*, which revives the salacious original.

1960s The Classics are given the distinctive black jackets that have remained a constant throughout the series's various looks. Rieu retires in 1964, hailing the Penguin Classics list as 'the greatest educative force of the 20th century'.

1970s A new generation of translators arrives to swell the Penguin Classics ranks, and the list grows to encompass more philosophy, religion, science, history and politics.

1980s The Penguin American Library joins the Classics stable, with titles such as *The Last of the Mohicans* safeguarded. Penguin Classics now offers the most comprehensive library of world literature available.

1990s The launch of Penguin Audiobooks brings the classics to a listening audience for the first time, and in 1999 the launch of the Penguin Classics website takes them online to a larger global readership than ever before.

The 21st Century Penguin Classics are rejacketed for the first time in nearly twenty years. This world famous series now consists of more than 1300 titles, making the widest range of the best books ever written available to millions – and constantly redefining the meaning of what makes a 'classic'.

The Odyssey continues …

The best books ever written

PENGUIN ⊕ CLASSICS

SINCE 1946